John Forest Norman
"
1947

What Jesus Was Like

WHAT JESUS WAS LIKE

or

ASPECTS OF THE PHYSICAL LIFE OF JESUS

Zacchaeus . . . tried to
see what Jesus was like
St. Luke 19 : 3 (Moffatt)

BY

G. ERNEST THOMAS

GREAT NECK, NEW YORK

WHAT JESUS WAS LIKE

Copyright 1946
By
PULPIT PRESS

First Edition

Printed in U. S. A.

TO MY
FATHER AND MOTHER
WHO SHOWED ME
WHAT JESUS WAS LIKE

FOREWORD

AT one point in the New Testament it is said that "Zacchaeus . . . tried to see what Jesus was like." So, too, have countless other men and women in every generation. The Christian faith has played such an important part in the development of civilization that untiring efforts have been expended in learning more about the Author of the faith.

The addresses in this volume are an attempt to gather together the meager knowledge available concerning various aspects of the physical life of Jesus. They were written under the pressure of a world torn by war's aftermath, and were delivered as a part of a regular pulpit ministry.

Most of these messages were presented during the season between Ash Wednesday and Easter. It is during Lent that the average Christian is moved by an eager longing to know more about Jesus of Nazareth.

I am aware of the debt I owe to others upon whom I have drawn freely for illustrative material. I should like to make special acknowledgment to the following:

To William L. Stidger for permission to quote his poem, " Judean Hills."

To Amos N. Wilder for permission to quote his " I Have a Heart that Cries for God."

To Dodd, Mead & Co., N. Y., for permission to quote from H. V. Morton's " In the Steps of St. Paul."

To Donald Ross for permission to quote his " God Be Praised."

I am greatly indebted to Miss Esther Pierce, my secretary, for her tireless efforts in the preparation of the manuscript, and to my wife for her counsel and encouragement.

G. ERNEST THOMAS

Haddonfield Methodist Church
Haddonfield, New Jersey

CONTENTS

What Jesus Was Like

CHAPTER I

The Face of the Master

Text: "For God, who commanded the light to shine out of the darkness, hath shined in our hearts, to give the light of the knowledge of the glory of God in the face of Jesus Christ." — *II Cor. 4: 6*

A SERIES of brief biographies was published a few years ago by Hendrik van Loon. He employed a unique method to make his word portraits seem more real. Imaginary banquets were prepared to which he invited a number of famous guests. Beethoven and Bach, Washington and Napoleon, Shakespeare and St. Francis,— these and many others came from centuries past to take their places at the banquet table, unhampered by the handicap of time and space. The author allowed his readers to see their faces and hear them speak.

Suppose such a banquet were to become a reality! Suppose it were possible to bring back the great of other days so that we might see and hear them! There are millions of Christians who would plead that Jesus of Nazareth be the first invited guest. Men of every age have dreamed of a time when they might see the face of Christ.

[1]

The Scripture tells almost nothing about the physical characteristics of Jesus. There are many passages like that in St. Mark 10:21 in which the writer says, "Jesus, looking on him, loved him." Such a verse tells something of the inner character of Jesus — His tenderness, sympathy, and interest in human beings — but it answers none of the questions concerning His physical appearance. How tall was He? What color were His eyes? What color was His hair? What were His features? These and many other questions have remained unanswered through countless generations.

It has been difficult for many Christians to understand why the Disciples did not leave a picture of the Master for future generations to see. Many earnest followers of Christ have declared that those who loved Him should have sought out the world's best sculptors and painters to record the appearance of their Lord. But the Disciples lived in a world in which statues of Roman and Greek gods were displayed on every hand. Few villages, however small or far removed from the larger cities, were spared ornate representations of the gods. The Second Commandment was deeply engraved on Hebrew minds. It made images of Jehovah seem revolting. And the idea of physically portraying Jesus of Nazareth was no less abhorrent. The thought of preserving for posterity the physical characteristics of Jesus in parchment or stone was probably never given serious consideration.

But Paul writes to the Church at Corinth about "the light of the knowledge of the glory of God in the face of Jesus Christ." The face of Jesus Christ! It intrigued Paul. And questions concerning the face of the Master have both puzzled and inspired men of every age.

II

Several objects having an association with the face of the Master have been preserved for many centuries in famous religious shrines. During the Middle Ages some of them enjoyed a reputation of dating back to the time when Jesus was on earth.

The relics are now browned and rotted with age. They were once supposed to bear the imprint of the face of Christ. They include Veronica's Veil, which is now in St. Peter's in Rome, the "Volto Santo" in Lucca, and the Holy Shroud in Turin. Most famous of all is the cloth which Christ is said to have sent to Abgar, the pious King of Edessa, after having left on it a miraculous impression of His face. All of these are accompanied by legends telling how the imprint of the face of Jesus was left upon them. Sometimes St. Luke or Nicodemus is credited as the artist.

The relics do not satisfy a seeker for truth. They give no acceptable knowledge of the face of the Master. They were born of superstition, and were often fostered by men who sought to increase the authority of a particular shrine. They leave the Christian unsatisfied. There is nothing in them which explains the victorious song of St. Paul concerning "the glory of God in the face of Jesus Christ."

III

The first attempts to picture Christ which have been preserved to our day were made about the year 200 A. D. By that time Christianity had a vast following in the Greek and Roman worlds. The pagan converts to Christ did not hold the same ideals which inspired the early Christians. They had been educated to worship many gods who were youthful in appearance and athletic in form. It is easy to understand, then, why they portrayed their Lord as a beardless youth of strong physique. Scores of such representations of the Master have been preserved in the catacombs of Rome, and in some of the ancient temples. The pictures are primitive in form, and almost entirely lacking in spiritual meaning for the Christian of today.

About the year 350 A. D. a new manner of portraying Christ came to be widely used. Under the Emperor Constantine, Christianity had been recognized as the state religion of the Roman Empire. No longer was Christ the champion of the meek and lowly. He became the mighty ruler of the world. Artists portrayed Him wearing magnificent robes, and seated

[4]

on a throne. A crown graced His head. He frequently held a scepter in His hand, and was adorned with jewels and other precious stones. In that stage of the development of sacred art there was little or no attempt to reflect more in the face of Christ than might appear in any conquering ruler. Character and spiritual strength were of no importance. Indeed, in many of the portraits of Christ dating from that age, the face of the Master seems to have been copied from statues of the Emperor Constantine. What a parody on the Man of Galilee! Such pictures must have left Christians with no understanding of what Paul meant when he spoke of "the glory of God in the face of Jesus Christ."

A little later another change can be noted in the manner in which artists tried to paint a likeness of the Master. It grew out of an increased recognition of His authority by educators and scholars. Many of the finest schools were changed from pagan institutions to schools for Christian meditation and study. Thus it was that, during the fourth and fifth centuries, we often see Christ pictured as a teacher, seated among the scholars and philosophers. Almost always He held the Holy Book on His knee. In such paintings Christ himself is represented as a philosopher. He has a curly beard, customary for teachers of that day. He is older in appearance than the more youthful representations which were left in the catacombs.

Some of the fourth and fifth century portraits or statues attained a high spiritual plane. Most of the artists, however, were driven by the sole purpose of arguing that Jesus was a teacher of philosophy. Their work does not give a satisfactory understanding of the face of Christ.

With the coming of the Reformation another change can be noted in the way Christ was portrayed. Fostered by a world which had developed a new interest in spiritual truth, the finest artists attempted to paint a likeness of Jesus. Many of them were abject failures. Many of their works are repulsive to the modern Christian. However, in those important years certain physical characteristics of the Master came to be accepted by every artist. Jesus was made to appear youthful, yet with the dignity of godliness. He was often pictured with a short beard. His dress became the white, flowing robe which is even now associated with Palestine. But of even greater importance was the approach to His facial features and expression. The artists studied the Scriptures. They sought to understand His inner strength of character. They tried to reflect His sympathy and understanding. They labored to put the conception of the Son of God into a portrait of the Son of Man. Often the artists failed to reach their goal, but their achievements have increased immeasurably our understanding of the Master. Every Christian would be poorer if he had not been blessed with a heritage which includes the face of Christ as portrayed by Raphael, Titian, Da Vinci, and many others.

In recent years religious artists have made further studies of the Gospel records. Through the insight which such studies have given them they have been able to put on canvas an even more satisfactory face of the Master. Perhaps the most familiar of the modern paintings is Hoffman's "Christ in Gethsemane." One day more than a hundred portraits of Christ, by artists of every age, were placed upon a table in a church school room. The minister talked with a congregation of junior boys and girls about the painters who have tried to portray the face of Jesus. Then he asked them to examine the pictures on the table, and to choose the one which seemed to them most nearly like the Master as they thought of Him. All except one in the group picked Hoffman's "Christ in Gethsemane." It was evident that the artist had caught the "glory of God as revealed in the face of Jesus Christ."

Hoffman is not the only modern artist who has tried to satisfy the human yearning to look into the face of the Master. Holman Hunt in his "Light of the World," Zimmerman in his "Christ and the Fishermen," and, more recently, Sallman in his "Head of Christ," have given form and life to the spirit of the Master. Long centuries ago Ovid wrote:

Often a silent face has voice and words.

[7]

Such a fact is frequently true of pictures of Jesus. The silent portrait reflects what the heart has long expected to find.

IV

Yet the mind of man which desires earnestly to see the face of Jesus does not depend alone on the work of the painter or the sculptor. Great and helpful as are their contributions to the life of the Christian, they are not the only source of authority. There are other ways by which the face of Jesus can be known.

First, a deep spiritual awakening is often accompanied by a clear conception of how Jesus looked when He labored in ancient Galilee. Scholars have expressed doubt as to whether the Apostle Paul ever saw Jesus during His earthly ministry. Many students of the Bible have maintained that Paul's failure to mention such a meeting with Jesus is clear evidence that he did not know the Master before the Resurrection. But no one knew Jesus so well, or spoke more confidently concerning "the face of the Master." Paul had known Him through a spiritual experience. It was enough to satisfy his every need.

Millions of Christians, farther removed by time and space from the earthly life of Jesus than was Paul, have had a similar experience. Many seekers after truth who were lonely for God have come to a high hour of faith. In that hour the Master was present in

[8]

their hearts. From that moment they knew how He looked!

I know a family which has always kept a place at the dining table for Christ, the Unseen Guest. The children grew up with the daily reminder of the Presence of the Master. No picture or sculptured masterpiece is needed to tell them what He was like. He is alive in their minds and hearts.

Just as Christ walked the road from Nazareth, and made His claim on the lives of the fishermen by the Sea of Galilee, so He often walks the roads of the world. He enters churches and homes, and challenges the human soul. For all those who have known such an experience, the face of Christ is made real. The poet has eloquently described how it happens in these words:

I had walked life's way with an easy tread,
Had travelled where comforts and pleasures led;
    Until one day, in a quiet place,
    I met the Master face to face.

With wealth, and power, and fame for my goal,
Much thought for my body, but none for my soul,
    I had entered to win in life's great race,
    When I met the Master face to face.

I met Him and knew Him, and blushed to see
That His eyes full of sorrow were fixed upon me,
    And I faltered and fell at His feet that day,
    While my castles melted and vanished away.

[9]

Melted and vanished, and in their place,
Naught else did I see, but the Master's face,
    And I cried aloud, " Oh, make me meet
    To follow the steps of Thy wounded feet."

My thought is now for the souls of men,
I have lost my life to find it again,
    E'er since that day in a quiet place,
    I met the Master face to face.

This experience does not belong solely to the mystic. It can and does happen in the lives of people of every class and clime. Common people with eager hearts are able to see " the glory of God in the face of Jesus Christ."

Second, the face of the Master can often be observed in the lives of those who have caught His spirit. Paul wrote to the church at Philippi challenging his Christian friends to " let the mind be in you that was in Christ Jesus." When the mind of Jesus makes its claim on a life, the reality of the experience can often be seen in that person's face. Shakespeare wrote:

    There's no art
To find the mind's construction in the face.

The mind of the Master in a man or woman brings out qualities which hint of what the face of the Master was like.

I know a little girl whose mother read to her each evening a story from the Bible before tucking her into bed. One evening the little child spoke up suddenly as the mother was giving her a good-night kiss. "Mummy," she said, "I know what Jesus looked like." "What did he look like, dear?" the mother asked patiently. The child threw her arms around her mother's neck. "He looked like you, Mummy! Just like you!"

There is something profound in the words of the child. She had been hearing of Jesus: of His works, of His kindness to children, of His healing of the bruised and suffering people. The child's mind had groped for something within her own experience which would tell her what Jesus was like. And she thought of her mother! Her mother was full of good works; her mother was kind; her mother could soothe and comfort when there was pain. The face of the Master was real because she knew someone who was like Christ.

The lives of countless Americans have been enriched by the legend of the Great Stone Face as written by Nathaniel Hawthorne. It told of a boy who lived in the shadow of the Great Stone Face. He dreamed of a day when a man would come to their village with a face which would reflect the calm and peace of the Man of the Mountains. Years passed, and the dream was unrealized. Yet his hopes never faltered. At last he was an aged man, and disappointed because his expected hero had never come. One day a visitor to the village looked at the old gentleman in amazement. "Why, sir!" he shouted. "Your face is exactly like that of the Old Man of the Mountains!" The one who had dreamed so long of a face to match the mountain had wrought such a likeness in himself.

The same miracle is often repeated in the lives of faithful Christians. Followers of Christ dream of the day when they may look into the face of the Master. Day by day their lives are given to the following of His teachings, and to fellowship with Him. It is then that the miracle occurs. The face of the Master is reflected in them. Others with lesser faith may pause for a moment before a consecrated Christian life, and then go away saying, "Now I know what Jesus was like!"

Jesus lived and died in far-off Judea. No sculptor or painter made a permanent record of His appearance; no writer of the Gospels paused to give even a single sentence to tell His followers how He looked. But the face of the Master still inspires the noblest aspirations of man. Much remains to be known. Yet millions of His followers gladly confess their faith that "the knowledge of the glory of God" was revealed "in the face of Jesus Christ."

CHAPTER II

The Eyes of the Master

Text: "Blessed are your eyes, for they see." — *Matthew 13: 16*

THE eyes of Jesus have always held a fascination for those who were eager to know how He looked when He lived in ancient Galilee. Students of the Bible have often speculated about His vision. Artists and sculptors have reserved their finest skill for a portrayal of His eyes.

The human eye is an important key to an understanding of character. In the pictures of the pitiable refugees of many nations who are the innocent victims of war, neither the tattered clothing nor the emaciated bodies gives the most eloquent testimony to their tragedy. It is their eyes which reflect a tale of misery and suffering such as could not be compressed into a volume of words. The eyes are the windows through which we see their broken hearts.

The biographies of great men abound with references to their eyes. No other quality is mentioned so often. Every biographer of Savonarola, the mighty monk of the Middle Ages in Italy, speaks of his piercing eyes. One writer describes them as "eyes of fire." John Wesley had flashing eyes which served him well on many occasions when he was pursued by a mob. One writer says, "No crowd could long retain its anger before his snow-white hair, and eyes which looked into their very hearts." Abraham Lincoln's eyes influenced almost all who knew him. Some who recalled meeting the Civil War President dwelt on his height; others on his plainness of feature. But almost every writer reserves the rarest adjectives to tell of Lincoln's eyes. Walt Mason wrote:

> Sad eyes that were patient and tender,
>   Sad eyes that were steadfast and true,
> And warm with the unchanging splendor
>   Of courage no ills could subdue!
>
> Eyes dark with the dread of the morrow,
>   And woe for the day that was gone,
> And sleepless companions of sorrow,
>   And watchers that witnessed the dawn.
>
> Eyes tired with the clamor and goading,
>   And dim with the stress of the years,
> And hallowed by pain and foreboding,
>   And strain by repression of tears.
>
> Sad eyes that were wearied and blighted,
>   By visions of sieges and wars,
> Now watch o'er a country united
>   From the luminous slopes of the stars.

Lincoln's eyes reflected his deep sympathy for the victims of war. Within their depths we read the agony which he felt for a nation sorely divided. And with it all there is the hope that a new and better land may come out of the struggle. It was the eyes of Lincoln which told the story of the man and his dreams.

The Gospel writers say nothing about the physical characteristics of the eyes of the Master. The nature of the land from which He came makes it almost certain that they were dark. A few artists have portrayed Him with blue eyes. They attempt to reflect the universality of Christ, but their portrayals are hardly in keeping with what we have reason to expect in a Galilean of the first century.

In the New Testament the indirect references to the eyes of the Master are numerous. What He said about the eyes of others, and what He Himself saw with His eyes tells His followers much more than could be gained by a mere description of their physical properties.

I

The eyes of the Master looked with interest upon ordinary people and common things. The Christ of God might easily have been so concerned with eternal matters that there was no room for the affairs of every day. History records the story of many individuals who, thinking they had a special contact with the Creator, have not deigned to stoop to the simple problems of humanity. They considered such interests as beneath their dignity. With Jesus it was different. His eyes were always seeking out common men and simple things.

His joy in the insignificant was a continual embarrassment to His followers. They could not understand why He stopped to look into the faces of little children. They were impatient when He gave freely of His time to the woman of Samaria. They never ceased to wonder why He paused to notice the mustard seeds, the sparrows, the woman sweeping anxiously to find a lost coin, or the boy with the three barley loaves and two fishes. His eyes searched out the little things which others passed by without seeing.

It is a tragedy that the followers of Christ miss so much of the simple grandeur of everyday life. I knew a gracious lady who kept a spirit of youthfulness until she was past ninety years of age. When the automobile came into general use she welcomed it as a new friend, and insisted on learning to drive. She not only took pleasure in riding in airplanes, but she seriously pressed her relatives to allow her to learn to fly. But it was in her human relationships that her sense of expectancy was best seen. She welcomed each new generation of children as if they were her own. She shared the experiences of children as if she were observing them for the first time. Toys always seemed to give her as much pleasure as they gave the boys and girls. Ninety years was no handicap to halt her from inventing new games and stories to enchant little ones. She had come close to a discovery of the fountain for which Ponce de Leon searched so long. She exemplified the spirit of perpetual youth.

Too many of us begin to feel superior, and take on a continually bored air with the passing of childhood. With Wordsworth we can say:

> Little we see in nature that is ours;
> We've given our hearts away, a sordid boon.

Eyes that are blinded to simple pleasures and satisfactions miss many of life's greatest joys. The Master lived His happiest hours when He shared the everyday pleasures of common people. It is that same awareness of the countless, ordinary gifts of the Creator which even today provides His followers with the "joy which passeth human understanding."

In a discussion of the physical characteristics of the human eye, an article in the *Encyclopedia Britannica* explains why some people's eyes seem to sparkle. The author declares that feelings of joy or sadness tend to increase the flow from the tear-ducts. These tears are brushed over the eyes by the natural habit of blinking. It is their reflective power which seems to give them a sparkle.

Eyes that notice simple beauties — a bird on the wing, a hidden flower, the shape of a snowflake, or a baby's smile — are eyes which the Master would praise. They are eyes sparkling with quick sympathy and appreciation.

The people upon whom Jesus looked with interest are a reminder to His followers that common folk are God's first concern. The list of those to whom Jesus gave special attention includes only a few who could be classified with the wealthy or influential. There was the rich young ruler, Nicodemus, the centurion, the ruler with the sick daughter, and a few others. But the most of His time was spent with the needy by the roadside, or the sick in the market-place. His eyes wandered no further than the place where human need was greatest.

Happy people are not necessarily those who travel to the far corners of the world, or who spend a large portion of their lives within halls of learning. They are not always those who can awaken with a feeling of complete material security. The joy of the Master is found in eyes that are continually seeking out experiences which give opportunity for service, or which provide a moment of laughter. Men who peer constantly at pictures of those whom the world calls great, and who long for a life which provides equality with the mighty, are not those who find happiness. It is in sharing the joy in the lives of common people that men still discover their richest rewards. The eyes which see such values are like the eyes of the Master.

The eyes of Jesus also peered into the distance. They saw the small and tender things of every day, but they gazed far beyond to eternal values and purposes.

George Cornicelius in his painting, "Christ Tempted by Satan," expressed unforgettably that factor in the vision of the Master. He painted the eyes of Jesus red with loss of sleep, and with weeping over the blindness of men. The masterpiece has been described as follows: "The subtle mystery of the Temptation story is not explained, but portrayed in the expression of the eyes of Jesus. They seem to look, not at you, not through you, but past you into infinite abysses as His mind judges, weighs, and tests the principles and conclusions that throughout future years are to direct His actions and conduct."

The Gospel record gives added weight to the assertion that the eyes of the Master seem "to look, not at you, not through you, but past you into infinite abysses." Consider the incident when Mary Magdalene so narrowly escaped death by stoning. Jesus knew the moral failure and degradation of her life. Her sordid sensuality was as clear to Him as it was to those who carried the stones. But Jesus saw into her heart. He looked into the face of Mary and recognized not only fear, but a dissatisfaction with life as it had been. He saw her trembling, not merely in terror at the immediate consequence of her acts, but in horror at the degraded principles which had dominated her life. The eyes of the Master looked much further than the outward circumstances.

The power of the Master to see beyond the obvious is dramatically revealed in the incident of the lunatic among the rocks. On that occasion He saw what others saw. He was aware of the wild, matted hair. He noticed the self-inflicted wounds. He, too, could see the brandishing arms which threatened destruction for all those who went near the man. Yet He saw more than this. He looked into the lonely heart of the fugitive. He saw a spark of sanity there which might change him into a worthy man of God. He looked beyond the poor victim as he appeared on the outside to see the man he might become. When others fled away in wild terror, Jesus remained to speak words of encouragement, and to bring him back from the vale of despair. The eyes of the Master saw more than appeared on the outside.

It is that long view of life which distinguishes the followers of Christ from non-Christians in the world about them. Others are satisfied to draw their conclusions from the facts as they appear on the surface. Christian eyes look into the inner heart of every situation.

That the Master looked far beyond the present was demonstrated most perfectly during the last days of

His life. There was desolation for anyone who saw only the stark tragedy of Holy Week. Forsaken by His followers, forgotten by His friends among the common people, and victimized by a cruel and angry mob! And beyond the people stood the hard and remorseless Cross! The cold realities of the event are clear to us. They were no less clear to the Master. But there was a difference with Jesus. His eyes saw deeper than the Trial and the Cross to the effect of those events on the men He loved, and, in days ahead, on those who hated Him. His eyes took the long view of the pressing events. He looked far ahead to the hour when men would speak of the Triumph of the Cross.

It is in hours of tragedy that the long view is most needed by faithful Christians. To weigh values on the strength of the facts as they appear in the immediate present is certain to result in disaster for the human soul. The eyes which see afar, on the other hand, will always mark a new day of hope after the long night of suffering.

Several years ago a fierce hurricane swept a wide path of destruction across the New England States. Mighty forests of lordly pine trees toppled over as if they were pins in a bowling alley. In that hour there were many who questioned whether the Creator had not, momentarily at least, forgotten His world. The eyes recorded only a tale of meaningless destruction.

Now the years have come and gone. I walked recently across one of those hillsides. Where once the green pines were spread in hopeless destruction there now is a vast treasure of berries. But that is not all! Cedars seeded themselves almost as if by the hand of a planter. Thousands of them are now three or four feet high. The years ahead promise a rich treasure for mankind in that once desolate country.

It is only those seeing the far distances who can know the Providence of God. Tragedy is never as devastating as it appears in a moment when its first blow is felt. In that hour the human tendency is to see only what is close at hand. The far look will bring a proper perspective to life. It was that power to take a far look at His world which characterized the eyes of the Master.

III

In the Sermon on the Mount, Jesus said: "The lamp of the body is the eye: if therefore thine eye be single, thy whole body shall be full of light. But if thine eye be evil, thy whole body shall be full of darkness." More than any other part of the body the eye, for the Master, was the key to the true nature of a man.

At no single point does our vaunted Western civilization stumble as when these words are realistically faced. Within our crowded cities there are millions of people who have few experiences during any week which give strength to the soul. The eyes look upon

[22]

newspaper headlines, crowded streets, and the artificiality of the modern movie. Many fail from week to week to see spreading fields or mountain heights, or to wing a way across miles and centuries through the magic of a great book. The "lamp of the body" sees nothing which can assure the pilgrim along life's highway that "thy whole body shall be full of light."

The concern of the Master is not only for those whose eyes look upon evil things. His words of challenge are spoken even more often to those of us who do not use our eyes at all. "Having eyes, they see not," He said. This is our condemnation, that God gave men power to see, and our eyes are unused. Jesus paid a great tribute to His disciples when He said to them, "Blessed are your eyes, for they see. . . ." Jesus considered the eyes of men as an undeveloped treasure house.

A blind American naturalist made a unique contribution to American thought. Clarence Hawkes, following an accident, had one leg amputated when he was ten years old. Three years later he was totally blinded by an accidental gunshot. In spite of his handicaps he wrote more than fifty books about nature during his lifetime. In describing this remarkable achievement he said, "As a boy I stored up on photographic plates within my mind many thousands of pictures of brooks and woods, birds and flowers. They were developed in the dark room of my soul, and still remain clear and beautiful. . . . Blindness has made it evident to me that my work in life is to teach other people how to see."

"Blessed are your eyes, for they see." The Master was aware of how meagerly God's greatest physical blessing to the individual is used. Mighty wonders of His world are forever lost to millions of people because "they see not." Glories in individual lives — hidden kindnesses, valiant endeavors — go unnoticed when His followers do not see with eyes like those of the Master.

Phillips Brooks has taken his place with the greatest preachers in the history of American Christianity. St. Gaudens' statue of Brooks in Boston has immortalized him as a strong, stern, and inspiring man of the pulpit. But Brooks was more than that. The stories of his kindness to the poor and helpless are beyond number. Booker T. Washington remembered how Brooks stopped to help him when he was a tiny colored boy, wandering helplessly on the streets of Boston. Others have testified that those in need who went hesitantly to his study, hardly daring to take the time of so busy a man, found a friend in him whose generosity of time and money was unfailing. The eyes of Phillips Brooks never failed to search out the places of greatest human need.

Jesus coveted such "eyes that see" for His disciples. He desired that the gifts of the love of God should be recognized by His followers. He wanted those who bear His name to notice the needs and longings of common people. That high summons is no less necessary today. Christians of this generation must live so nobly that they too can hear a whisper from the silence which says, "Blessed are your eyes, for they see."

IV

Artists still strive to set on canvas the eyes of the Master. It is probably true that no fully satisfying picturization of them will ever be made. They are eyes that see little things; they are eyes which, as Byron said, "look to the very soul"; they are eyes that look afar. They are eyes that challenge, and eyes that condemn. They are eyes soft with sympathy, and yet hard with condemnation of evil. They are eyes which look on the whole world, but they are eyes also which look at the individual. Nowhere in all the Gospels does the divinity of Jesus cry aloud its unmistakable truth as clearly as in the reference to His eyes. The eyes of the Master are like the eyes of God.

CHAPTER III

The Ears of the Master

Text: "He that hath ears to hear, let him hear." — *Matthew 11: 15*

THE sensitive ears of Jesus often detected a whisper in a babble of human voices. He frequently overheard without difficulty the conversation of individuals in the great throngs that crowded about Him. It is clear that His acute sense of hearing was no less remarkable than His other physical qualities.

Jesus revealed a deep concern for the hearing of His followers. He referred many times to the ears in terms which suggested that He held them to be one of life's most precious possessions. The importance, however, was in the fact of hearing. Deafness was a tragedy because the miracle of voices and sounds was lost to the individual. "Blessed are your ears," He said, "for they hear." He constantly expressed concern because words of truth were spoken, and yet they went unheard. Matthew Henry wrote that "none are so deaf as those that will not hear." It was that group of people who received the stern rebuke of the Master. He was both discouraged and angered by the people who "hearing, they hear not."

Mark records an incident in which a deaf man was brought to Jesus in the hope that he might be cured. The Scripture tells us that Jesus "took him aside from the multitude privately, and put His fingers into his ears . . .; and looking up into heaven, He sighed." Scholars have often been puzzled by the inclusion of the two words, "He sighed." Why did Jesus sigh? He was about to lift a burden, not alone from a man who was deaf, but from those who loved him. Yet Jesus sighed! The passage can best be understood in the light of the frequently expressed attitude of Jesus toward the power of hearing. He must have wondered when He looked into the face of the deaf man what the man was going to hear after he was cured. He must have wondered if he would join the vast company of those who "hearing, they hear not." It was that doubt concerning the use which would be made of the new-found hearing which led the Master to sigh.

Jesus was always listening for messages to the soul of man. At times He became impatient with those who heard only the humdrum sounds of the material world. "He that hath ears to hear, let him hear," He said. Across the centuries His voice continues to plead for us to respond to the summons of God.

The blessings of hearing still receive their most eloquent example in the use of the ears of the Master. Three characteristics of His hearing stand out in the

Gospel narrative. The same qualities should prevail in the lives of His followers in every generation.

I

The ears of the Master were attuned to catch the cry of humanity. The voices of those who were in high position in the life of the synagogue or the state held no fascination for Jesus. He deliberately chose the companionship of the lowly. The sound of fishermen at their nets, or workers in the fields, or women at the village well were the sounds He liked best to hear. Such concern for common people was not in itself a necessity. It was not demanded by His lowly background as a carpenter's son. He walked and talked easily with men of high position. Indeed, the Roman centurion and the highly-influential Nicodemus stood before Him with a humility which they usually reserved for a king. Even Pilate dropped his regal manner when he was confronted by Christ. The Master had an inner power which could have commanded the following of the mighty of the earth. That He cared not at all for the splendor of positions of social and political might has only served to emphasize His divinity. He turned His ear away from the trumpet which proclaimed the coming of a conqueror to listen to the low cry of humanity.

The voices of men who were in physical pain never failed to bring a response from the Master. Matthew tells of a day when Jesus was walking along the road near Jericho. "A great multitude followed Him." They pressed about Him. Some ran ahead to places which were slightly elevated so that, from the position of vantage, they might see Him more clearly. Caught in the midst of the pressing multitude were two blind men. They were sitting by the roadside. As Jesus passed by they cried, "Lord, have mercy upon us, thou son of David." Their voices were almost lost in the continuous babble of sounds which came from the crowd. But still they cried out in desperation and despair. It was then that Jesus came to a sudden stop, and called for silence. He had heard their plea for help. The Scripture records that their highest hopes were fulfilled that day. They were made to see.

The incident here was repeated over and over again. No amount of adulation could deafen the ears of Jesus to the call of human need. Sometimes we are given a glimpse of the Master weary and worn by the pressure of a crowd which would not release Him. But weariness did not deafen His ears to the needs of men. The ears of the Master were always attuned to catch the "slow, sad music of humanity."

It is easy for the followers of Christ in a new and different world to forget the example which His life so clearly presents. The cry of humanity can easily be interpreted as the repetitious and wearisome mumbling of the ignorant. The mad intensity of a song of despair from an army of unemployed men and women can become the wailing of those who will not work. In the personal realm, the deafness to human need can become no less tragic. The cry of physical pain can very simply be interpreted as "a work of the imagination" by those who will not hear. The sob of a child who has lost its mother is very easily dismissed with a quick, "He'll soon get over it," by those less sensitive to the hurts which plague mankind.

This generation has witnessed as much individual suffering as has any single generation in the history of the Christian era; and more, we pray, than any generation will ever be called upon to bear again. Modern war has taken its greatest toll in the lives of women and children. New and terrible implements of destruction are so designed as to spare the lives of the soldier at the expense of the cities and their flooding humanity. What cries are arising from those who are hungry, homeless, and bereaved! A loving God will need great mercy to forgive those of us whose ears are deaf to the wail of suffering which rolls as a mighty wave across the globe. Again the quiet voice of the Man of Galilee whispers down the ages, "He that hath ears to hear, let him hear."

But the summons to serve suffering humanity is not simply a matter of giving and sharing the bounties which are ours. The personal satisfaction which comes to the giver is enough reward for the service. But there are further riches of glory for those with ears to hear the cry of human need. Jesus invited His followers who had well served their fellow men to "Come, . . . and inherit the kingdom prepared from the foundation of the world." It's a kingdom of eternity, but its beginning is in the present. Joy is the reward of service!

Dr. Henry C. Link in his "The Rediscovery of Man" tells of a lady who had recurrent periods of severe mental depression. An important position in a bank enabled her to be economically independent. She had little to worry her. But she could not escape despondency. When she became ill her physician recommended two weeks of rest and change in New York City. There she would hear good music and plays and, in some measure, recuperate. But after a time the escape from the home environment no longer provided the necessary cure. It was then she made an appointment to consult a psychiatrist. He suggested that, instead of going to New York, she become interested in the families of the people with whom she worked; that she discover means of helping her neighbors; and that she try to serve others. The lady followed his advice. She attuned her ears to hear the cry of humanity. Service became her motive in living. Dr. Link records the fact that the recurring illness was completely cured.

The truth in the Gospel is as dependable today as it was when Jesus walked by the Sea of Galilee. Men and women who hear the call for help which comes from those in need are the men and women who receive the inner fortitude and strength essential to every time of crisis.

The ears of Jesus were always open to the call of people in need. His followers likewise should be worthy of the tribute, "Blessed are your ears, for they hear."

In the second place, the ears of Jesus were open to hear discouraging and hard words. There came a day when His earthly ministry no longer won the enthusiastic support of the common people. In spite of the miracles of healing and the words of Eternal Life, the crowd turned away from Him. It was a difficult day for the disciples when they told Him that the common people were no longer interested in Him. The harsh words of failure must have been difficult for Jesus to bear. Someone less filled with godliness might have determined to leave an unappreciative humanity to its well-deserved fate. But Jesus listened to the words of discouragement. He heard out to its end the sad and sorry tale of human weakness. Then He moved forward to the Cross.

The words of scorn and hatred which were hurled at Him during His trial and crucifixion were accepted in a similar manner. His ears missed not a single disparaging shout. Even until the time of the actual crucifixion He might have escaped. Human and divine hosts were awaiting His summons. There were enough friends from the Galilean countryside to have carried out a sizable revolt. His life might have been saved. But the jeers and scornful laughter were accepted as part of the price He paid to win the souls of men. He heard every bitter word without flinching.

It is a common quality in human nature to desire to turn away from unpleasantness. The ear is easily closed to words and ideas which make for insecurity, or which stir the conscience. It is always simpler to run away from a constant reminder of responsibility than it is to face the situation in all its stark realism.

The teachings of Jesus have often fallen on ears which were immediately closed to His strong challenge. It was so at the time of His earthly ministry. There are several incidents recorded in Scripture similar to the one in which we read, "Many of His disciples, when they heard this, said, 'This is a hard saying: who can HEAR it?'"

The Sermon on the Mount contains teachings which cannot be heard by the sensitive Christian without their creating an uneasy feeling of personal failure. The words of the Master concerning personal morality, love of enemies, and the need for a complete trust in God must leave even the most faithful Christian with a consciousness of much which has been left undone. The words are revolutionary in their challenge for both individual and social living.

Thackeray, aware of the words of Jesus, said, "He that hath ears to hear, let him stuff them with cotton." Many ears have been symbolically "stuffed with cotton" as a protection against the "harsh sayings" of Jesus.

The world will never reach the goal so perfectly portrayed in the conception of the Kingdom of God until there is a widespread acceptance of the teachings of Christ. A physician in an Eastern city declared recently that he went to church on Sunday morning expecting to find there a pillow on which he could rest his weary head. It must be admitted that the Church has a mission to provide the spiritual rest and comfort which are sorely needed in our mad world. But that is only one of its functions. It has as well a mighty task to proclaim the way of God to salvation through Jesus Christ. In presenting Christ, the Church has the responsibility to present Him in all His glory. His words, however strange to our way of life, must be shouted so loudly that the farthest ear may be reached. If such words disturb and create uneasiness with life as it is, then we will need to remember that they are Christ's words, and His way of eternal hope.

A minister, paying tribute to an earnest Christian in his congregation, had intended to say that the man was a pillar of the Church. Unfortunately, he declared instead, "He was a pillow of the Church." There are all too many "pillows" in the Church of our day. They are earnest men and women. They make ardent sacrifices to keep alive the glory of the existing organization. But a reminder of the simple teachings of Jesus causes the hearing to fade, and an impassable wall to be erected between the listener and his God.

Our generation needs a new legion of the faithful who will hear to the end the challenging teachings of Jesus. Such a legion will not reply, "This is a hard saying: who can hear it?" Instead there will be a proud shout, "This is a hard saying, I can hear it!"

III

In the third place, the ears of the Master were attuned to listen to the voice of God. He heard not only the voices of men, but the "still small voice" of His Heavenly Father. On many occasions we see Jesus leave the companionship of the Disciples for the solitude of the night. Out under the stars He could both listen, and talk to God. The fruits of that fellowship are evident in His works, and in the manner of His teaching. The intimacy of the relationship between Father and Son is eloquently proclaimed throughout His earthly ministry.

The noise and furor of our world make it difficult to accustom the human ear to the voice of God. It is said that continuous work in one section of a great steel plant, where mighty hammers make thunderous sounds, affects so severely the ear drums of the laborers that a whisper can never again be heard. The continuous roar of passing traffic on a busy thoroughfare makes it difficult to hear the rustle of the garments of God. The shattering fury of a modern "swing" band makes it hard to attune the ears to the song of angels' choirs. On every side there are artificial sounds which tend to deafen the ears of men to the whispers of eternity.

For nearly two years the church bells of England were silenced. Their tolling was reserved for an hour when the invader should set foot on British shores. It is said that people shouted for joy when the bells rang again. Strong men and women, who had borne without flinching the destruction of their cities, now openly shed tears of joy. For the people of England the pealing of the bells in the church towers was the voice of God. All the roar of planes and the bursting of bombs had not closed their ears to that voice.

Nothing in our world must be allowed to deafen the hearing of Christians to the "still small voice" of God. There must be frequent occasions when the

[36]

ears are trained to receive the sound waves which roll in from above.

The American Indian has been famed for his acute hearing. It is said that footsteps or animal treads could be heard far away by Indians with particular skill. Mary P. W. Smith, an authority on early Indian lore, gives an interesting description of an Indian boy's training. His remarkable hearing was not merely a hereditary gift. It was cultivated by careful practice. As a small boy he identified a rap against a tree, first at a distance of one hundred yards; then he learned to recognize it farther and farther away as his hearing improved.

By such careful training each one of us may learn to recognize the voice of God. Our civilization will crumble if we listen only to a babble of human sounds. We need in this generation to attune our ears to hear messages of eternal importance. The fate of man in the world demands it.

There is a legend concerning a Bishop of the Church of England. He had been reading and saying prayers all his life. But he had never cultivated the "listening ear." Once there came an hour of tragedy when his life foundations had crumbled. In desperation he went to the altar of the church, and there fell on his knees. From his heart he cried out, "O God!" The silence was broken by the voice from on high which said, "Yes, my son, what is it?" The Bishop was so startled by the unexpected answer to his prayer that he fell dead before the altar.

Countless Christians are deaf to the voice of God. Our ears never become attuned to catch the flood of eternal song. Vast treasure stores of spiritual strength and power are forever lost to God's people because we have not learned to hear the wisdom spoken from the heart of a loving Heavenly Father.

IV

The ears of the Master were alert to catch both the cry of humanity and the whisper of eternity. He looked into the faces of those who followed Him with an eager hope that they, too, would learn to use the divine blessing of hearing. Again in our day He is challenging His followers. Harken to His words: "He that hath ears to hear, let him hear."

CHAPTER IV

The Hands of the Master

Text: "Except I see His hands. . . ." — *John 20: 25*

AMONG the recorded incidents following the Resurrection of Jesus there is none more familiar than that in which Thomas appears as the central figure. He was absent when the Risen Lord made His visit to His followers who were gathered in an upper room in Jerusalem. He missed the splendor of the hour when the doubts of the Disciples were dispelled. When Thomas entered the room he found his companions completely transformed. Their sorrow had been changed to joy. The solemn air of watchfulness had left them. No longer were they silent men. They were eager to tell of a change which had come within them. Words tumbled one after another from the clamoring voices. All tried to be the first to tell the wonderful news. When at last they were hushed into silence, Thomas spoke aloud his doubts. "Except I see His hands . . .," he said.

It is strange that Thomas should have placed so much importance upon the Master's hands. He did not say, "Except I hear the voice of the Master."

Nor did not say, "Except I see His face." It was the hands of Jesus which this doubter desired most of all to see.

There must have been something eloquent about the hands of Jesus. They are referred to, either directly or indirectly, forty-five times in the Four Gospels. There are more references to the hands of Jesus than to any other of His physical attributes. A student of the Bible cannot avoid the conclusion that the hands of the Master had a strange fascination for those who were close to Him.

In many respects the world does not change. The doubters of this generation, and men who stand on the outer edge of the Christian fellowship, still say to those who proclaim the Christian faith, "Show us your hands!" Such people do not care a great deal about the voice of Christians, and the arguments which are presented to demonstrate the truth of various creeds. They are not interested in the appearance of Christians, as to whether followers of Christ are different in dress or position from other men. More than anything else they desire to see Christian hands.

It might seem dangerous to place too much significance on human hands. Jesus intimated that the hand is a secondary organ of the body. "If thy right hand offend thee, cut it off," He said. Someone has declared that the hand is only the servant of the mind. Because of that fact it is easy to think that hands are

[40]

of small significance when compared with the whole individual. But in a larger way the hand is symbolic of the man. What the hand does in a large measure tells what the man is. The world today still looks toward the faithful Christian and says, "Except I see your hands. . . ."

I

What was it that Thomas expected to find in the hands of Jesus? First, he knew that he would see hands marked by suffering. He wanted to gaze upon the nail prints, symbolic of the agony upon the Cross. Those ugly wounds, he thought, would demonstrate definitely that the wondrous guest was his Risen Lord.

Men today still look for the marks of suffering in the hands of faithful followers of Christ. The Christian religion is the religion of sacrifice. It summons men to a life of service for others. No greater tribute was ever paid to the Christian way of life than that which came from an Army officer who had been stationed for twenty months in China. He said, in an interview, that he had on many occasions seen people designated as Christians. "Look," someone would say, "that man is a Christian." He added that every such mention of a man being a Christian excited the native Chinese. An eager look of hope came into their eyes. For the suffering humanity in China the very mention of the word "Christian" raised possibilities that sacrificial service would be forthcoming.

[41]

During the terrible days of the French Revolution the final test of aristocracy was an examination of the hands. People of wealth and position were dragged before the citizens' tribunal. Their prison-dirtied faces and tattered clothes did not mark them as different from their accusers. But when their hands were examined the tale of their past lives was revealed. If their hands were soft and free from callouses, then they were condemned to death on the guillotine.

Christianity today is on trial throughout the world. As never before in all its history, people are weighing the true worth of the Faith. Words in themselves are no longer convincing. Men are tired of words! The larger test is that of deeds. Men today who are persuaded to accept the Christian Gospel hope to see in the hands of the followers of Christ the same marks of suffering which Thomas saw so many years ago. "Except I see His hands. . . ." The world today looks for Christian hands to be marked by suffering.

II

In the second place, Thomas expected the hands of Jesus to be clean hands. He had looked upon the Master's hands many times. They were unsullied by the foulness of the world. As He had lifted them before His followers, Jesus' hands came to symbolize a kind of purity not found in other men.

In this respect also the world has not changed. Men today still expect the Christian to hold clean hands before the world.

One day I stood at the bedside of a woman who was dying of a dread disease. She seemed to find comfort in those last moments of agony by holding fast to my hand. She breathed her last breath while tightly gripping my hand in hers. As soon as it was possible I went to a nearby washroom. Deeply moved by the horror of the scene I had just witnessed, I washed, and washed, and washed again. No amount of water and soap seemed to cleanse the hands of the contact with disease and death.

There have been many who have returned from an hour when ideals were permitted to tumble in the dust, and who desired to wash their hands. They have washed and dried, and washed again without the satisfaction of feeling really clean.

It was in that spirit that Judas Iscariot rushed into the presence of the Elders clutching his grimy pieces of silver. They burned his hands. The dirt seemed to penetrate his very flesh. When he held out his hand, it was as if he preferred to be separated from the instrument which had accepted the blood money. His agony of spirit was revealed in the mumbled confession, "I have betrayed innocent blood." Judas was a man who knew the horrible experience of having unclean hands.

Shakespeare caught the horror of unclean hands in his portrait of Lady Macbeth. Her mind had planned murderous deeds, but it was her hand which had accomplished them. All the guilt of humanity across the ages is revealed in her endless rubbing of her hands together as if to wash them clean, while she cried: "Out, damned spot! out, I say! . . . Here's the smell of the blood still: all the perfumes of Arabia will not sweeten this little hand."

Carl Sandburg in his "Abraham Lincoln: War Years" makes the drama of Lincoln's death a masterpiece of poignant tragedy. One can never forget his picture in words of the flight of John Wilkes Booth from the theater in Washington. We are permitted to share the relentless pursuit. When the chase comes to an end, and Booth is caught, we accompany those who carried the traitor to a nearby porch. In his last moments Booth whispered, "Tell my mother I died for my country." After a period of silence he spoke again, "I thought I did it for the best." Finally he gazed at his hands. In that moment a look of agonized despair crossed his face. With superhuman strength he raised himself from the pillow. He lifted his hands and held them with the palms up. Then he whispered, "Useless! Useless!"

In Lady Macbeth and John Wilkes Booth there is pictured the tragedy of the ages. Hands that are unclean! The hands have become symbolic of the inner and real self.

Thomas, the doubter, desired in the Upper Room to see the hands of the Master. He knew that they would be clean hands if it were truly his Christ. The doubting world of today looks as never before at the hands of Christians. If they are not clean hands, representing clean thoughts and clean acts, then the unbeliever raises his voice to cry, "Hypocrite!" It matters not whether they be hands of one who has great and mighty responsibilities in his community, or if they are the hands of a humble man whose influence never goes beyond his own home, the cry is still the same. "Except I see His hands . . ." and they must be hands that are clean.

III

In the third place, the Doubting Disciple expected the hands of the Master to be marked by service for others. Roland Hayes, the great Negro tenor, has amazingly expressive hands. His glorious voice is eloquent. But the movement of his hands is hardly less a tribute to his genius. His hands often tell a complete story of the words which he is singing. In a similar manner the hands of Jesus revealed completely the message He had come to proclaim. Thomas had looked upon those hands on many occasions. He had seen them as they had touched the eyes of the blind, or were raised in benediction over the five thousand on the mountain. They were hands accustomed to serving others. Thomas was sure that he could recognize his Lord by the appearance of His hands.

In a similar manner people in every century have looked at the hands of those who were called Christians, expecting them to be hardened by service for others.

Many of the foremost artists of this generation have poured their best talents into portraits or sculpture of human hands. They have recognized the significance of the human hand as revealing what was in the heart. Not the least effective of these is the painting titled "Praying Hands," by Albrecht Durer. Even more impressive than the painting itself is the setting out of which it came. As a youth Durer had dreamed of becoming an artist. When he left home, he was penniless. At Nuremberg, Germany, he found a man somewhat older than himself who also desired to study art. They shared a room, and painted together. When their money was gone, and it seemed that they must give up, Durer's friend made a suggestion.

"This way of working and trying to study," he said, "is intolerable. We are neither making a living, nor are we mastering our art. Let us try another way. One of us can earn the money for our daily bread while the other continues to paint. Then when the paintings begin to sell the one who has worked may have his chance."

"True," replied Durer thoughtfully, "it is a good plan. But let me be the one to earn money for our bread."

"No," the older friend answered positively, "I must be the one to work. It is better so. I already have a place of employment in a restaurant. I am older, and have not as much talent as you. You must not waste your years. Let it be as I say."

The older man had his way. Durer labored faithfully to perfect his art while his friend worked at any kind of labor to buy them food and to pay for the garret room. He washed dishes, scrubbed floors, and polished brass. His hours were long and the work was hard, but he did it cheerfully. He was helping his young friend, while he looked forward to the time when he would be able to paint again.

At last the day came when Durer sold a wood-carving. It was sufficient to buy food, and to pay the rent for a considerable length of time. He rushed home to share the good news.

"Now the time has come when I will earn our bread!" he shouted proudly. "You shall go back to your paints, my good friend. You need no longer work, for I will care for both of us."

So his friend left his serving, and dishwashing, and

scrubbing, and took up his brush. But something had happened during the months when he had labored so hard with his hands. The work had stiffened his muscles, enlarged his joints, and twisted his fingers. They could no longer hold the brush with mastery and skill. He struggled long and hard, only to find that his dream of becoming an artist had been sacrificed forever.

When Durer learned what had happened to his friend he was filled with great sorrow. Shortly after this Durer returned one day to his room unexpectedly and heard his friend's voice speaking an earnest prayer. He entered softly and saw the work-worn hands folded reverently as he knelt by the bed. Durer determined to catch the expression of faith in the hands, and put it upon canvas.

Durer's "Praying Hands" is a masterpiece. It reveals volumes about the human soul. One need not look beyond the hands for a face. Both face and mind have been given expression in the gnarled hands.

Every individual needs to ask himself frequently what story his hands relate concerning his true self. Many hands merely tell of an ability to apply artificial make-up. Such hands could not be used for washing children's faces or pouring out a life in days of active service. In my hearing a man said, rather proudly, that his hands had taken such a shape that he could do two things perfectly; he could hold a cigar, and deal playing cards. The man was joking, of course! But there was enough truth, also, to give many Christians a reason to think seriously. It is a tragedy if the story told by human hands is nothing more than a life devoted to a selfish search for pleasure.

IV

In the Upper Room in Jerusalem there was a sudden silence. The Disciples were hushed. The door had opened, and Thomas had entered the room. Then the silence ended quickly! Voices were raised, one after another, in wild enthusiasm. Each Disciple sought to outdo the others in telling of the glorious experience of seeing the Risen Lord. Thomas was unmoved: "Except I see His hands . . ." he said. Jesus' hands could reveal the truth of the Resurrection for the Doubting Disciple. Only by the hands of the Master could all the mysteries be cleared. They were the key.

The hands of His followers are still the key to Christianity's answer to human need. The world today, as skeptical and uncertain as was the Doubter of old, still looks eagerly toward the followers of Christ. It listens with growing interest to the talk of the "Kingdom of God." Then, with bated breath, it says, "I want to believe. It's what I need, but . . . except I see your hands."

Chapter V

The Feet of the Master

Text: "The Lord stood by me, and strengthened me."
— *II Timothy 4: 17*

Judean hills are holy,
   Judean fields are fair,
For one can find the footprints
   Of Jesus everywhere.

One finds them in the twilight
   Beneath the singing sky,
Where shepherds watch in wonder
   White planets wheeling by.

His trails are on the hillsides
   And down the dales and deeps;
He walks the high horizons
   Where vesper silence sleeps.

He haunts the lowly highways
   Where human hopes have trod
The Via Dolorosa
   Up to the heart of God.

He looms, a lonely figure,
   Along the fringe of night,
As lonely as a cedar
   Against the lonely light.

Judean hills are holy,
  Judean fields are fair,
For one can find the footprints
  Of Jesus everywhere.

It was with words of such splendid beauty that
William L. Stidger described the manner in which
the footprints of Jesus were indelibly left in ancient
Judea and Galilee. Many visitors to Palestine in the
last decade will voice a protest against what seems a
distortion of the facts. Modern Palestine is not a land
of natural beauty. Its mountains and hills are largely
a barren wasteland. Jerusalem, Nazareth, and the
smaller villages are places of outward filth and ugli-
ness. Then, too, the civil war between the Arab and
Jewish populations, striving for superiority, has made
it difficult for the modern pilgrim to Bible lands to
capture the spirit of the Christ. Bloodshed, turmoil,
and degradation — these are prevalent in modern
Palestine.

But even now a stranger in the Holy Land cannot
entirely escape the presence of Christ. Bethlehem,
Nazareth, the Sea of Galilee, Jerusalem, and many
other places sacred to His memory still weave a magic
spell about the eager seeker for truth. The presence
of an army of occupation to control the warring fac-
tions only serves to recapture the conditions of life
which prevailed during the days when Jesus walked
the earth.

Far removed from the time of the earthly life of Jesus, it is still possible to feel His presence in the land where He spent His earthly days. The feet of the Master have left indelible marks in ancient Palestine.

Only a short time after the Resurrection, the followers of Jesus began to speak with positive assurance about His presence in cities and villages far distant from the place of His earthly ministry. St. Paul in his "Letters" returns constantly to an emphasis of that truth. In Second Timothy 3:11 he says: "The Lord stood by me, and strengthened me." Christ had left the print of His feet in the way which Paul had walked.

In the magnificent defence which Paul made before King Agrippa, the reader is impressed no less by the manner of the speaker than by the words he spoke. His face was alight with a bright candle of faith. His whole demeanor was not that of a prisoner, but a conqueror. And why? Paul does not hesitate to explain the reason for his power. It goes back, he declares, to the day on the Damascus Road when he came to know for himself the presence of the Christ. The Master left His footprints on the road which Paul had travelled.

The miracle has been repeated many times during the history of the Christian Church. Men and women have known the presence of the Master in places of danger, or in hours of sorrow. Young people have been strengthened to do what is right by a presence divine. Millions of faithful Christians have been able to say in triumph with St. Paul: "The Lord stood by me, and strengthened me." Such lives demonstrate what it means to have discovered the footprints of the Master.

I

Almost every Christian home has its reminders of the presence of Christ. It may be a motto to tell the members of the family that "Christ is the head of this house; the Unseen Guest at every meal; the Silent Listener to every conversation." It may be a picture of Christ. Prints of Da Vinci's "Last Supper," Hoffman's "Christ in Gethsemane," and Plockhorst's "The Good Shepherd" have been distributed widely, and have found a hallowed place in Christian homes. But more often than these there is the influence of the Holy Bible. In many homes it remains on a parlor table with the family knickknacks and mementoes of a vacation journey. But it is there! And the Bible is a perpetual reminder of spiritual realities which, though often neglected, have been the foundation for the home. It is in these symbols of religious faith that the footprints of the Master are found in the dwellings of Christian families.

A recent number of the *Kiwanis Magazine* included an editorial written for fathers. It quotes a modern father as saying: "I don't know what's the matter with my children. They must be dumb. They object to attending church for two hours on Sunday. Of course, I don't go to church; I'm busy reading the paper. The children leave their clothes about the house, no matter how many times I tell them to put suits and coats away. Of course, my clothes are left anywhere; but then, I'm tired when I get home, and can't be expected to care for such things. The children don't seem to realize that tobacco and alcohol are dangerous for them. Of course, I use tobacco and alcohol, but I'm older and can control the amount I consume. The children put their elbows on the dining room table in spite of constant reminders from their mother. Of course, I put my elbows on the table; but I'm older and do it without being awkward. Yes, it's hard to understand why my children are so dumb. They can't understand that what I tell them is only for their own good."

This bit of satire in a secular publication reveals a sensitiveness to right and wrong; a rare sense of fair play; and a conception of the importance of fatherhood. Christ had left His footprints on the life of the man who wrote it. Because of that fact his home is forever different.

Thomas Paine frequently made scathing attacks on organized religion. His unhappy and lonely childhood left a permanent mark on his life. God was a stranger, and eternal verities were never secure to this disillusioned individual. But he spoke of the American home as "the palace of the colonies." Mr. Paine was correct in his recognition of the large place which the home played in the beginnings of the United States. He neglected to take the further step in admitting that a living and vital faith in God was the foundation for the American home. The footprints of the Master were found in the wilderness and by the sea. It was the Divine Presence in American homes which gave the country its strength.

Paul's words can be spoken today with confidence. "The Lord stood by me, and strengthened me," he said. The footprints of the Master have been left in Christian homes.

II

The feet of the Master have left their prints on the streets of the cities of the world. Church spires are a pledge to every stranger that there are people in that city who recognize a call for loyalty to the Man of Galilee. Nor are the churches alone in reminding men of the ever-present spirit of the Master. A large proportion of the hospitals in America were established by philanthropic men and women who were acting in the name of Christ. The public schools and other civic institutions had their genesis in a concern for the welfare of people. That concern resulted from a knowledge of the teachings of the Master.

Some months ago I listened to the twenty-fifth

annual report of the Family Welfare Society in a New England city. The report sketched the history of the Society from its modest beginning. It pointed to the year in which certain projects were organized. The first playground was established within that period. Free milk for children of poor families had been a recent development. The plan for summer vacations for city children desperately needing fresh air was started fifteen years before. Here was a record of idealistic service which demonstrated a vital interest in human values! Then I turned to look at the Director of the Program and the Trustees of the Society. Every one of them was a person of religious faith and purpose. They were men and women who one day had come to know the Christ, and the joyous way of service to which He challenged His followers. It was clear that the footprints of the Master had been left in that city.

III

It is not only in American cities and homes that the presence of Christ is known. The prints of His feet can be seen in lands and churches far different in custom than those familiar to the average American.

Palestine is a land foreign to most of us who live in the Western Hemisphere. It is foreign, not alone in flag, but in customs as well. The Eternal Creator was moulding a plan to fit the ages when Christ was born in that obscure and unimportant land. There were few people to nationalize Him there. Yet they attempted to do so, and might have succeeded if He had not strongly resisted their efforts.

Christ left His footprints in old Judea; and in the homes and cities of present-day America. It is clear, then, that He can leave them anywhere in the world. There is no land where His feet cannot tread, and no people who cannot hear His voice.

The presence of Christ has reached far beyond our native land. His influence has been felt in nations with strange manners of life, and in churches with customs of worship which are far removed from the simple forms of American Protestantism.

During the First World War three American prisoners escaped from a German prison camp. One of them was wounded as he fled, and had to be hid by day and carried through the night by his companions. At last they sought out a tiny French parish church to ask for refuge and help. An aged priest answered their repeated knocking and, when he recognized them as Americans, immediately led them to a place where they could be safe from enemy searching parties. But the joy in their temporary safety was dispelled by the condition of their wounded companion. He grew weaker during the night, and died in the hour before dawn. Before continuing their flight, the Americans desired to see their comrade buried with such honors as were possible in that enemy-held

[57]

land. They asked the priest if a plot was available in the cemetery at the rear of the church. "Was the soldier a Catholic?" asked the white-haired holy man. "No," they answered, "he was a Protestant." A look of sadness came over the priest's face. "Ah, it is unfortunate," he said, "for only Catholics can be laid to rest in this cemetery." Then he brightened. "But we can put him yonder just outside the fence." He pointed to a quiet and secluded spot. The soldiers agreed that a place near the fence would be acceptable. And so it was done! While they watched from the window in their underground hiding place, their companion was laid to rest outside the main portion of the cemetery. When the service was over it was easy for the young Americans to see that the priest was not satisfied. He pleaded with them to remain a little longer and share his meager food and refuge. Wearied as they were, they decided to stay in hiding for another night. The following morning they looked out again for the last time toward the place where their comrade had been laid. A strange sight greeted them! During the night the fence which had separated their friend from the cemetery had been removed. Now the fence went around his grave in such a manner that his body was within that hallowed place. Turning to ask the priest for an explanation, they found him standing close by them. A smile of triumph was on his face. "A Protestant may not be buried in the cemetery," he said, "but there is no rule which says we cannot move the cemetery to include a Protestant."

People are different all over the world. National characteristics, age-long customs, and many other factors contribute to emphasize those differences. But these are not a barrier to the presence of Christ. He left His footprints in many lands, and among many differing peoples. Americans are only a small segment of those in the world who can say with confidence, "The Lord stood by me, and strengthened me."

IV

These words have a message for the individual Christian. Paul tells his readers that "The Lord stood by ME, and strengthened ME." It was his own life, as well as the community life, which felt the power of the divine presence. Such an experience is true in our day. The footprints of the Master have been left on the road we are trying to follow.

It is not merely chance that countless Christian leaders testify to the fact of divine guidance. John Wesley wrote in his "Journal": "I do not remember to have felt lowness of spirits for one quarter hour since I was born. I see God sitting upon His throne and ruling all things well." George Washington wrote in a letter to a friend, "We can always count on the goodness and mercy of God."

[59]

Life is often lonely in the struggle for the right. It sometimes appears that we are fighting a solitary battle for better things. Milling crowds hurry along the level road of self-satisfaction. The road away from idealism and uprightness is often cluttered with an onrushing mob. But the upward path, the road to the Christian goal, is frequently an unused highway.

It was while walking that path that Paul said, " The Lord stood by me, and strengthened me." When Jesus had lifted the high challenge of the Christian life before His disciples He did not say, " Go that way." Instead He looked into their faces, and said, " Follow Me!" He had left His footprints on the road which He called upon His followers to take.

A life governed by Christian idealism leaves many disciples of Jesus with a feeling of separation from neighbors and friends. There is an inevitable loneliness when the rushing crowd passes us by in a search of lesser values. Yet we are not alone! Robinson Crusoe's feeling of despair disappeared when he found footprints on the sand. They told of the presence of another member of the human race. There is a far greater encouragement for the follower of Christ. We struggle upward on life's journey! The way is difficult and lonely. But we are always encouraged by the footprints of the Traveller who has walked ahead of us. The feet of the Master have left their marks on the highway we are trying to follow.

CHAPTER VI

The Power of the Master

Text: "The whole city was in excitement over Him."
Matthew 21: 10 (Moffatt)

ORGANIZED religion seems drab and uninteresting to many people. Its rituals and ceremonies do not capture a vital interest. The tendency of the Church to concern itself with what they think are minor matters often alienates those who have large civic and world responsibilities. By way of contrast early Christianity was a religion which was vitally alive. In one passage, speaking of Jesus, it was recorded that "the whole city was in excitement over Him."

What was the source of the enthusiasm which ran through the city like a tidal wave when Jesus came? Was it the physical appearance of the Master? Could it have been His powers of oratory? Important as they were, they do not explain the extraordinary impression which He made upon people.

More than anything else it was what Jesus could do which caused the excitement. Word had been carried far ahead concerning His strange and wonderful power. Common people had heard of His deeds; His ministry of healing; His mastery of human weakness. The story of His power had spread afar. People in towns and villages in every part of Palestine were talking of the Galilean whose touch was able to change lives. They waited expectantly for new demonstrations of His power. No wonder "the whole city was in excitement over Him."

The power of Jesus has not dimmed with the centuries. In every age a breathless excitement has swept through cities and countries wherever His message has been proclaimed. Sometimes decade after decade went by without a people discovering the full possibilities of vital Christian faith. Then a St. Francis, or a Luther, or a John Wesley found again the mystic power which came to the early Church. Once more a trembling excitement gripped a needy people, and "the whole city is in excitement over Him."

The power of the Master to satisfy human needs and longings is no less an assured fact for expectant people in our day. In every phase of our corporate and individual life there is nothing more essential to our continued progress than a rediscovery of the mighty power revealed in the Man of Nazareth.

I

The power of the Master is essential to the world in this hour when human foundations have been

shaken as never before in history. This is the generation when false powers have been sought after by vast
multitudes of people. Millions of Germans looked
to Hitler for their security. The people of the Soviet
Union placed their hopes in the power of a material-
istic Communism to satisfy all their needs of life. In
England and the United States we have attempted to
develop a liberalized democracy as the answer to the
questions and uncertainties of our changing civilization. In 1939 much of the civilized world resorted
again to war as a means to settle pressing human problems. Slowly the fact has become clear to people in
Italy and Germany, and the United Nations as well,
that the use of war to heal the sickness of mankind is
a dangerous experiment. It destroys and maims life.
It leaves a trail of suffering in the lives of innocent
victims. Its power to glorify a state or to strengthen
the character of a nation now has become merely an
empty mirage. People all over the world are eagerly
seeking for another answer to human longings. The
question becomes insistent: why not try the power of
the Master?

In the year 220 Cyprian, Bishop of Carthage, wrote
to his friend Donatus a letter which describes eloquently the manner in which the Christians of that
early century were made strong by the power of Jesus.
He wrote: " This is a cheerful world as I see it from
my fair garden, and from under the shadows of my

[63]

vines. But if I could ascend some high mountain, and look out over the wide lands, you know very well what I would see. Brigands on the highways. Pirates on the seas. Armies fighting. Cities burning. In the amphitheaters, men murdered to please applauding crowds. Selfishness and cruelty, and misery and despair, under all roofs. It is a bad world, Donatus, an incredibly bad world. But I have discovered in the midst of it, a quiet and holy people who have learned a great secret. They have found a joy which is a thousand times better than that of any of the pleasures of our sinful life. They are despised and persecuted, but they care not. They are masters of their souls. They have overcome the world. These people, Donatus, are Christians, and I am one of them."

Those unacquainted with the manner in which the early Christians changed their surroundings might think that the Power they found in Christ was an escape from the world of misery, and a refuge from its chains. But it was far more than that! Driven onward by the power of the Master, they sought to transform their world. Men who had caught the glory of the divine presence were never again satisfied to remain apart from the vale of human tears.

Think what might happen if it can be truthfully said of men in our day that "the whole world is in excitement over Him." A new and different kind of world peace will follow a widespread acceptance of the promise of Jesus concerning the peacemakers who are the children of God. Whole new vistas will spread out before the millions of victims of the horrors of war if the world is influenced by Jesus' promise that He came so men could have life, and have it more abundantly. Certainly an undreamed-of future will loom before all mankind if people in Russia, in Britain, and in the United States are excited over His challenge to "love your enemies."

Men have often dismissed religion as drab and uninteresting. But that has seldom happened when the spirit and teachings of Jesus have laid their claim upon a people. When that happens "the whole world is in excitement over Him."

II

There is need for the Christian Church to rediscover the spirit of the text. People in Jesus' day were discouraged with organized religion. The temple in Jerusalem no longer inspired the confidence of the people. The pride which they and their fathers had felt in the worship of Jehovah was gone. Dishonesty in the buying and selling of sacrificial birds and beasts did not go unnoticed by pilgrims from all over Palestine. Jesus lashed out with a whip and drove the money-changers from the temple. He was not alone in recognizing the dishonesty of the temple practices. The common people knew of it, and their confidence in their religion was undermined. They were aware that the best places and the highest honors went to those who possessed the greatest wealth. They felt the scorn which was heaped upon the poor. They were not blinded to the fact that those less worthy of a place in God's house were often given the seats of highest honor. It was that same prevailing hypocrisy which Jesus attacked in His parable of the Pharisee and the Publican.

To the people who were burdened by doubts concerning the worth of organized religion Jesus came with His message of hope. No wonder the poor folk of village and city were excited! The strange Galilean had a faculty for plunging to the heart of things to find what was real and true.

Jesus is able to work the same miracle in His Church today. He calls the leaders of organized religion away from the jealousies that undermine, and the bickerings that destroy. He touches the hearts of those who merely carry out forms and rituals. For all of us He seeks to light the torch of vital faith.

There have been many recent examples of the way in which the power of Christ breaks the barriers of jealousy in the mission fields of the Church. Christian denominations, which often worked in competition, have united their forces in many parts of the world. There is hope ahead that followers of Christ in foreign lands will not need to adjust themselves to a great variety of competing denominations and sects. When that hour comes there will be one great Church dedicated to the work of Christ. Such a Church can stand as a mighty force for good against the powers of ignorance and unbelief.

The same power is needed in the churches of our own country. It is a scandal of Christianity that we are divided into so many denominations and sects. Differences in theology, or manner of administration, or social customs have too long separated God's people! The greatest hour in the history of religion in America will dawn when the differences are set aside, and the faith which is common to all of us is proclaimed. It can then be said with truth: "The whole Church is in excitement over Him."

Is not this message also needed in the individual church? Strangers who come seeking spiritual security often turn away from the church in despair. Too often jealousy, and hatred, and desire for personal glory are evident in the deeds of the leaders of the organization. Such practices are not worthy of the name of Christ! There can never be petty disagreements in a church where the spirit of Christ is the guide and rule for the Christian fellowship. Those who by the power of leadership or wealth are tempted to usurp the important places will seek to have others receive the glory which they themselves have earned. On the other hand, people of small talents and abilities will give thanks to God that there are those who are able to give the leadership and guidance necessary to the progress of God's program on earth. There will never be reason for dissension and separation if the Master's spirit is present. It is certain that a new hour will dawn for every church bearing His name if it can be said, "The whole Church was in excitement over Him."

III

The conception of the power of the Master has a challenge also for each of us as individual Christians. It is to the individual that Jesus looks with deepest concern and love. He recognized that the hope of changing a city, a church, or a world is bound inseparably to the hope that individual men will be transformed by the power of His spirit. The world's hope, in its final essence, must wait for an hour when millions of men everywhere are "in excitement over Him."

Every faithful Christian is confronted by a question suggested by the phraseology of the narrative in the Gospel of Matthew. "What am I excited about?" probes the text. "What causes me to respond with the greatest enthusiasm to life?" Many people are excited about what appears in the morning paper. Some people are, and justly so, excited about the work which they are doing. Others throw the larger amount of their enthusiasm into the quest for pleasure. But think of what would happen if it could be said that the Christian people of America, as individuals, are "in excitement over Him."

The power of the Master, when it is allowed to have full sway in a life, invariably changes that life. The physiologist tells us that a heart which contracts is fatal to life. It is so with the soul. When a human soul shrivels through constant practices of selfishness and greed, desperate measures are necessary to restore spiritual life. It is at that point that the power of the Master is most necessary. Wherever there is excitement over Him, new life flows into the human soul. Such a life is transformed.

Recently I went on a journey by train. Hardly had the train left the station when a baby began to cry. It would not be consoled. As the train rolled mile after mile the child alternately sobbed and screamed. The mother was greatly upset by the baby's crying. Of course she was concerned about the child, but she was also anxious because the crying seemed to disturb the other passengers in the car. A look of disgust mounting to anger filled the face of a lady seated nearby. As the crying continued, the lady turned, and in a voice which carried far down in the car, she exclaimed, "Why don't you keep the child quiet?" Tears came to the eyes of the mother. She was desperate. Yet still the child kept on crying. It was then that a man arose from a seat not far away. His manner indicated that he was accustomed to travel. His dress spoke eloquently of worldliness. He stepped back to where the mother was trying in vain to make the baby happy. He spoke quietly to her, and in a moment he had taken the baby into his arms.

He walked to the end of the car, then turned and came back again. As he walked he sang softly! At first the baby seemed unmoved by the attention. She cried on! But after a time the sobbing grew less violent, then more faint, and at last it ceased altogether. An audible sigh could be heard all over the car. The man had found the secret, not only of how to make a baby happy, but he had proved that all of us were not like the prim, complaining lady. The humanity of every passenger had been vindicated.

There are many lives in which sympathy has no place, where love is forgotten, and in which service to others is considered a sign of weakness. In all such individuals the soul has contracted and may even be dead. On the other hand, a genuine excitement about the power of the Master is the herald of a new depth of sympathy for others.

The late Bishop Thorburn, one of the mightiest voices in Methodist history, went as a young man to India as a missionary. Shortly after arriving in Bombay he was entertained in the home of the presiding bishop. When he awakened in the morning he found his boots had been cleaned, and were shining with a gloss which came only from hard labor. Later he discovered that the bishop himself had polished his shoes. The incident brought home to him the power of the Master as revealed in the humble service of His followers. It became a beacon light throughout his ministry.

The enthusiasm for Jesus which reveals itself in changed lives and nobler purposes was never more needed in our world than today. A new hope will come to mankind when it can be truthfully said of His followers: " They were all in excitement over Him."

IV

The power of the Master to meet human need never fails. There have been times in the world's history when men have wondered if Christianity had lost its way in the changing civilization. Severe persecutions have given rise at times to the question of whether Christianity would endure. But always the power of the Master has found a channel of expression in the lives of faithful men.

Ibsen in his " Emperor and the Galilean " gave eloquent voice to the enduring power of Christ when he wrote:

" Where is He now? Has He been at work elsewhere since that happened at Golgotha?

" I dreamed of Him lately. I dreamed that I had subdued the whole world. I ordained that the memory of the Galilean should be rooted out on earth; and it was rooted out. Then the spirits came and ministered to me, and bound wings on my shoulders, and I soared aloft into infinite space, till my feet rested on another world.

"It was another world than mine. Its curve was vaster, its light more golden, and many moons circled around it. Then I looked down at my own earth — the Emperor's earth that I had made Galileanless — and I thought that all I had done was very good.

"But behold there came a procession by me on the strange earth where I stood. There were soldiers and judges and executioners at the head of it and weeping women followed. And lo, in the midst of the slow moving array was the Galilean, alive and bearing a cross on His back. Then I called to Him and said, 'Whither away, Galilean?' and He turned His face to me and smiled, nodded slowly and said, 'To the place of the skull.'

"Where is He now? What if that at Golgotha, near Jerusalem, was but a wayside matter, a thing done as it were in passing! What if He goes on and on, and suffers and dies, and conquers, again and again, from world to world!"

The power of the Master is available today. The gift which He alone can give is essential to the continued progress of civilization. When there is a wide acceptance of His power, the people of this generation will join those in ancient Palestine of whom it could be written, "The whole city was in excitement over Him."

CHAPTER VII

The Touch of the Master

Text: "And He touched her hand, and the fever left her; and she arose, and ministered unto them." — *Matthew 8: 15*

GREAT lives and mighty events have often been shaped by small incidents. Abraham Lincoln's hatred of slavery was born at a slave-block in New Orleans; the long and bitter War of the Roses broke out in all its fury when a hand plucked a red rose; Sir Walter Raleigh's life adventure began on a morning when a sailor, home from the seas, talked of strange people in strange lands.

Think of the touch of the Master! Insignificant, isn't it? But it played a part in many of the events of His earthly ministry. Compared with the look on His kindly face, the flash of His eyes, or the sound of His expressive voice, there is little here which would seem to inspire enthusiasm. But the record makes it clear that His touch was the means by which hope, faith, and power were brought into the lives of those in distress.

In the evening hour when Jesus entered the home, and found Peter's wife's mother sick with a fever,

"He touched her hand, and the fever left her." Matthew tells of two occasions when blind men pleaded for help. "Then touched He their eyes," and the miracle of human sight was restored. Mark tells of a deaf man whom Jesus touched: "He put His fingers in his ears." And of a man born blind, whom "they beseeched to touch him." Then Jesus "put His hand upon him," and the wondrous deed was done. It was an understanding of the manner in which the touch of Jesus brought life and hope to those in despair which led Jemima T. Luke to write:

> I wish that His hands had been placed on my head,
> That His arms had been thrown around me.

The touch of the Master was left in places where human misery and need called most urgently for help.

In writing his life of Jesus, Dr. J. Warschauer suggests that the Master used the sense of touch to secure greater confidence and faith from those He desired to help. Jesus emphasized on many occasions the necessity for faith. "All things are possible to him that believeth," He said to the father of a boy who was ill. It is well known to modern psychology that the touch of a hand often conveys sympathy or power more than argument, or pleading, or scolding. It was in the spirit of this truth that Jesus used so often the sense of touch. At least, of one thing we are sure, great faith was born, and miracles were accomplished by the touch of the Master.

There is no single mention in the Gospels of the imprint of the hands of Jesus apart from incidents in which He was helping people. He left no blot to mar the record of His perfect life of service.

As we look at the days between the temptation and the crucifixion in which His touch is again and again associated with deeds of loving service, the sensitive Christian will often question himself concerning where he has left the imprint of his hand. We look steadily at the places where Jesus' touch is to be found, and immediately we are driven to examine our own hands, and the deeds they accomplish. Something deep in human nature makes men want to pattern themselves after that which they admire. It is so with Christians. A look at the triumphant life of Christ, and something within us calls for a pledge of service. "We test our lives by Thine" are words of a familiar hymn. They reflect the normal and natural challenge to noble endeavor which Christians feel in the presence of the glorious life of Jesus.

The touch of a human hand is left in many places in the span of a single day. A recent news item told of a Nebraska judge who wrote to Mr. J. Edgar Hoover of the Federal Bureau of Investigation for information concerning fingerprinting. In his reply Mr. Hoover said, "It may interest you to know, judge, that on your letterhead you left thirty-six fingerprints, and on the envelope sixteen." There is something frightening in that picture! Fingerprints are left in an endless trail! The touch of a hand is recorded in all its deeds.

Men still speak in whispers concerning amazing scientific inventions which were developed during World War II. To the average man the word Radar still suggests an awesome mystery. But everyone was aware that something of shattering importance was born when we were told that an escorting cruiser could turn its Radar in a vast circle around the ship and pick up a few inches of submarine periscope as clearly as if it were an ocean liner. The power of Radar to magnify the insignificant is almost beyond the reach of our imagination.

But suppose an instrument could be developed which would recapture and magnify the fingerprints made by a Christian in a single day. There might be cause for glory in such a revelation! And perhaps shame as well! But no such invention is necessary for sensitive followers of Christ. The searchlight of our conscience is always looking back at a day, or a week, or a year to see where we have left our fingerprints. We are conscious of the marks left by our hands.

I

The touch of a Christian hand should be found upon a work that is worthy. It may be a farmer's hand

[77]

on a shovel or fork, or the shipbuilder's print on his tools, or a physician's hand on a fevered brow. A good mother who makes a palace of happiness out of her simple home, or a father who tries in honest toil to earn his daily bread,— these leave fingerprints at their work which are worthy of Christ.

A task that is honest, and which makes even a small contribution to the life of the human family, is worthy of the hand of the Christian. And, having such a work, we can go proudly about our way, knowing in the evening hour the peace which comes from the consciousness of a task well done.

The recognition of life's duties as God's work has seldom been expressed more eloquently than in a poem by Ronald Ross. Dr. Ross is an eminent scientist. He wrote the poem at the completion of long research in malaria. His discoveries were revolutionary. They promise relief for countless thousands of victims of that dread disease. He wrote:

> This day, relenting, God
>   Hath placed within my hand
> A wondrous thing; and God
>   Be praised. At his command
>
> Seeking his secret deeds
>   With tears and toiling breath,
> I find thy cunning seeds,
>   O million murdering Death!

I know this little thing
   A myriad men will save;
O Death, where is thy sting?
   Thy victory, O Grave?

Before Thy feet I fall,
   Lord, who made high my fate;
For in the mighty small
   Is shown the mighty great.

It is not given to every follower of Christ to make such a dramatic and worthy contribution to his fellow men. All of us, however, have a part to play in the whole drama of life. The touch of our hands at the close of a day's work should register a mark of service to God and to our fellow men.

II

The story-book detective steals quietly about the scene of the drama, carrying a magnifying glass. He makes a permanent record of fingerprints on furniture or windows. A "spiritual-detective" should be able to find Christian fingerprints wherever there is need for a sympathetic or helping hand. Someone wrote a novel titled "The Trail of the Scarred Finger." There are countless Christians who write a chapter each day in "The Trail of the Kindly Fingers." Their touch is continually left on the lives of people in need.

It is said that lilies were native to India. They were carried to England during the Fifteenth Century by the voyagers who had gone to the Far East in search of gold. The flowers proved a great treasure for the people of Britain. English gardens were soon famous for their beautiful lilies. When settlers were leaving England for the American colonies they took with them lily bulbs as a symbol of the beauty and refinement which they hoped to establish in the new world. So also did the pioneers, years later, who moved from the eastern seashore across the Alleghenys and into the West. Their wagon trains often carried boxes of lily bulbs. On the way the trains were frequently attacked by Indians. The red men plundered the wagons, but they saw no value in bulbs, and left them scattered by the wayside. There are now three great "lily belts" in America, and each of them is along a wagon route to the West.

A consecrated Christian life leaves a trail of kindly deeds in its wake! The fragrance of a life lived for Christ endures long after the work of a Christian hand has been completed.

Fingerprints are plainly left on what we read. The printed page easily catches and holds the record of a human hand. Many of us who are followers of Jesus would be embarrassed if our fingerprints on reading matter were magnified and recorded for posterity. The daily newspaper is often the only printed material which we find time for. Often the Bible bears no marks which tell of frequent use! Sometimes the occasional touch of a hand on the Word of God is well marked in the dust which has accumulated from weeks of neglect.

When He was a boy the Master must have studied Hebrew History. The Bible tells us that on a certain Sabbath Day Jesus read aloud in the synagogue from the Book of the Law. From the manner in which He quoted the Old Testament we know that He was on familiar terms with Moses, Isaiah, and the other great pioneers of the Hebrew faith.

Those who are trying to be followers of Christ in the Twentieth Century will leave often the touch of their hands on the Bible, the hymnbook, and other sacred literature. Contact with such sources of inspiration is essential for the power and guidance of those who are trying to carry on the work of the Master. The touch of a Christian hand belongs on that which is of God.

Latches and doorknobs often preserve a clear impression of the human hand. It is always to the doorknobs of a house that fingerprint experts give their most careful attention.

The enemies of the Master charged Him frequently with entering the houses of sinners. "See," they sneered, "He eateth with the publicans and outcasts." Yet Jesus did not protest! He was satisfied for His followers to know that His touch had been left on the doorknobs of the homes of those whom the world designated as outcasts. Praise still belongs to the followers of Christ who enter the homes of those who are poor and needy. Americans are too prone to test their social responsibilities by the size of the house, or the expensiveness of the furnishings of the people about them.

Jane Addams visited London as a young woman of twenty. While others in the party went to see the art galleries, Miss Addams spent her time in the slums and about the factories. One afternoon she entered a filthy brewery to find women carrying huge barrels of scalding-hot beer strapped to their backs. Her protest to the owner was answered by a curse. In that hour the life pattern for Jane Addams was set. The touch of her hand on the factory door led her to resolve to give her life for the relief of women and children. The exploited people of the world became her "family" and friends.

We never know when the opening of a door will bring the experiences and friendships which transform life. Roland Hayes seemed destined for a life of labor in a factory when he entered a tiny colored church in the South, and there met Arthur Calhoun. That night Mr. Calhoun told him he had a voice, and inspired Mr. Hayes with a desire to become a great musician.

Humble homes, poor and ill-equipped schools, and places where poverty has left its blight on life sometimes offer rich opportunities for those with eyes to see. They are the places which are sacred to the touch of the Master.

In contrast to the humble situations which ought to receive the imprint of Christian hands bent on service, there are other doors which followers of Christ should be ashamed to enter. I know of a lady who will not touch a doorknob outside her own home unless she wears gloves, or is otherwise protected against microbes. Germs are her horror in life! She carries her phobia to unreasonable extremes.

But there are doorknobs which no Christian hand should touch. Certain places of amusement are so foul that Christian fingerprints will bring cries of shame if they are magnified, and held up to the light of eternity. A visitor to Spain several years ago described a bull-fight as follows: "I felt nauseated. I kept asking myself why I had come. Later, at the hotel, I wanted to wash the eyes that had looked on that horrible spectacle." The tragedy behind those words lies in the fact that other visitors have been equally horrified by a first visit to a bull-fight, but have discovered that several successive visits gradually harden the sensibilities to a point where the cruelty and bloodshed no longer are construed as an evil.

Many amusements, which once seemed unworthy of the presence of a Christian, become acceptable by constant practice. The test of right and wrong is no longer as rigid as it once was. The list of what a Christian must not do has grown smaller with every decade. How, then, can the follower of Christ know where he should not go, or what he should not do?

The answer is not difficult. Let us think of our fingerprints as magnified and recorded in the pages of history. If we can face what is displayed there without shame, then we can be sure that the door may swing open wide, and we may be free to enter. The touch of the Master is the final test for those who are in earnest about their desire to follow Him.

III

The Gospel narrative tells of a woman who pressed forward in the crowd, reached forth her hand, and "touched the hem of His garment." The incident was given beautiful expression in a familiar hymn:

> She only touched the hem of his garment
>> As to his side she stole,
> Amid the crowd that gathered around him,
>> And straightway she was whole.

The suggestion here is appropriate to every life. We who are wise followers of Christ in this generation will often leave our fingerprints on the hem of His garment.

Much of modern civilization is crowded into large cities. In such places the pressure upon the individual is greater than at any other time or place in history. In such an environment the cultivation of the Presence of God becomes essential to victorious living.

One of America's outstanding physicians wrote recently concerning an experience of faith. The pressure of his practise had given him little time for thoughts of God, or prayer, or eternal truth. His crowded days had left him both spiritually and physically exhausted. In desperation he went to a place of spiritual retreat. There he lived for eight days a life far removed from the telephone, the newspaper, or the radio. He ate simple food, and retired early at night. He listened to lectures on spiritual matters, and read the Bible as he seldom had read it before in his lifetime. At the end of the eight days he relates that he went back to his work a different man. He had felt the touch of the Master.

Such a complete separation from the world and its demands is more than many of the children of the Twentieth Century are prepared to endure. Nor will this drastic measure be necessary if the soul is kept alive to eternal things by daily meditation and prayer. Every life needs the joy which comes from touching the hem of His garment.

Christ said, "Seek and ye shall find." True devotion will not go unrewarded. Wherever there is an eager longing to be in the presence of God, that life will know what it means to receive the touch of the Master's hand.

CHAPTER VIII

The Voice of the Master

Text: "Everyone that is of the truth heareth my voice."
— *John 18: 37*

A MINISTER startled a group of fellow ministers by stating that the public reading of the words of Jesus is the modern clergyman's most difficult task. His remark brought a smile to the faces of those who experienced no such difficulty. "What do you mean?" someone asked him. "The words of Jesus are easy to read; there are none that are difficult to pronounce." "It isn't the words that are hard," the speaker answered. "It's the voice that troubles me. When they were first spoken, the words of Jesus drew thousands of eager listeners. Yet today they make little or no stir in a congregation. It must have been His voice! I keep trying to read His words with an accent that reflects a portion of what He was able to impart."

Questions concerning the voice of the Master have often captured the interest and imagination of His followers. When a reader has been deeply moved by the fourteenth chapter of St. John it is natural that he should wonder with what tone and expression the words were first uttered. When the Parables have cast a spell over an eager reader, it is not strange that he should speculate as to the nature of the voice of the Master.

There is no treatise in the Gospels which describes Jesus' voice. There are, however, certain conclusions to be drawn from a study of the New Testament narrative. Seekers for truth can gather a clear conception of the voice which has instructed, comforted, and challenged His followers in every age.

I

First, the voice of the Master did not impress His hearers as a large and thunderous voice. Almost without exception the writers of the Gospels relate that "Jesus said," or "Jesus answered." There is little use of the words expressive of a loud voice. At the raising of Lazarus we read that "He cried with a loud voice." But these and two other references complete the exceptions. For the remainder, the words expressive of ordinary speech are employed by the writers.

Yet other persons in the Gospel narrative used the more explosive words. Two blind men "followed Him, crying out"; or again, "they cried out the more"; or "they cried out again." In the country of the Gadarenes, the man "cried out with a loud voice."

It is clear that the use of the words "said" and

"answered" to describe the speech of Jesus was not dictated by the limited vocabulary of the writers. They were acquainted with other words. But He did not leave the impression upon those who knew Him that He shouted, or screamed, or indulged in flights of oratory. He evidently was not the possessor of a huge voice.

A biographer of George Whitefield declared that "on a favorable day, people one-half mile away could hear his resonant voice." The late William Jennings Bryan is remembered as a man with a voice which seemed to roll through the surrounding hills. Such a voice did not mark the speech of the Master.

Because He had a soft voice does not mean that Jesus could not be heard, or that He was any the less effective in His speech. Abraham Lincoln did not have a big voice. Compared to Stephen Douglas his manner of speech was awkward. Yet his voice left an impression upon his listeners which could not be approached by the more dramatic Douglas. The experience was repeated at Gettysburg. Edward Everett possessed a voice of great beauty and strength. Yet the small voice of Abraham Lincoln won "The Perfect Tribute" from those who listened. In our own day the small voice of Miss Helen Hayes is well known. It throbs with such life and feeling, however, that it often seems to push back the walls within which she speaks.

Jesus used no voice which inspired His followers to think He shouted, or screamed. But it carried with such power that the five thousand massed on the mountain side listened in breathless attention through the heat of the day. Beyond the modest assertion that Jesus "said," or "answered," or "taught them, saying," there lies a voice of depth, and feeling, and power.

In the second place, we believe that the voice of the Master spoke with a beauty which was like music. Dante Gabriel Rossetti described the voice of a friend as "like the voice the stars had when they sang together." With such a beauty did the words of the Master reach out to challenge the lives of men.

The language which Jesus spoke encouraged musical voices. There were none of the harsh tones which characterize the languages of the western world. For the dweller in Ancient Palestine, even the most mundane things were described in soft phrases which were akin to poetry.

One day in the famous Blue Mosque of Sultan Ahmed in Constantinople I walked barefoot over the thick rugs to a far corner where an aged patriarch was reading aloud. A large audience sat before him on the floor with their knees crossed. They listened intently to his words. I realized that he was reading a language with which Jesus was familiar. The voice was soft and musical. It was nearer to song than it was to human speech. The language itself gave to the speaking voice a tone of rich beauty. In that moment I was swept across the centuries in imagination to a place by the Sea of Galilee where Jesus talked to His Disciples. His voice seemed to carry the same tones of soft and poignant beauty that came from the lips of the white-bearded old man in the Mohammedan mosque. I knew then that the very language which Jesus spoke was an indication that His voice had a beauty like that of noble music.

The words of Jesus as recorded in the Gospels give additional assurance that His voice had a beauty of expression. One cannot read aloud the Gospels in Greek ar Aramaic without sensing that the poetry of many of His words is comparable to any literature born in the mind of man. The translators of the King James' version of the Bible did an inestimable service to all English-speaking Christians by preserving the beauty of His speech. Only the dead of soul can read the Beatitudes without speaking with a voice which reaches outward for a song worthy of the words. It is so with the Parables of the Good Samaritan and the Prodigal Son. It is so with the fourteenth to the seventeenth chapters of St. John. The words of Jesus tell us that His voice had a sublime beauty of tone.

Third, the voice of the Master was sufficiently varied in quality so that it met every need of His busy ministry.

It had the soft charm which attracted children. Specialists in child psychology have declared that a tiny child responds more to the sound of a voice than it does to appearance. A stranger may be huge in size, and homely of face, but if his voice is kindly and understanding, the child will seldom cry out in fear.

Children heard the voice of Jesus, even when He was directing His words to men and women, and they pushed their way to be near Him. A small boy, evidently unaccompanied by his parents, remained close to Jesus throughout the long day on the mountain. It was on Him that the eyes of the Disciples were fixed when there was need for food. Children must have been attracted by His kindly eyes, but His voice was a factor in assuring them that they need have no fear in His presence.

His voice was sometimes raised in anger and indignation. One of the rare occasions in which the writers of the Gospels resort to stronger words than "Jesus said" to describe His speech occurs in St. John 12: 44. We are told that "Jesus cried and said, 'He that believeth on me, believeth not on me, but on him that sent me.'" At that time He was confronted by Pharisees who "loved the glory that is of men more than the glory that is of God." It was their refusal to recognize God's place in human life which stirred Him most often to anger. He could and did accept persecution, ridicule, and death for Himself, but for His

Father God He "cried out" in anger when there was lack of respect and honor.

The worldliness of men drew His strongest condemnation. It was as if He must speak with a louder voice because there was spiritual deafness. In his biography of an obscure French saint, John Oxenham tells the reader that Jean Marie had the habit of preaching with a loud voice, and praying in a voice that was hardly more than a whisper. He was asked why he did it. "When I am preaching, I am talking to men who will not hear anything except it be a loud voice," answered Jean Marie, "but when I pray, I pray to the God who hears even a whisper."

Jesus, too, lifted His voice in anger on the occasions when human arrogance and self-righteousness became a direct affront to God.

His voice had a quality of tone which reached the depths of human need. When proud Nicodemus came in the night to talk with the Master he listened to what seemed a strange message about the necessity for him to be "born again." The beauty of that hour of conversation is lost except we take into consideration the persuasive quality in the voice of Jesus.

Henry Wadsworth Longfellow spoke for countless followers of the Man of Galilee when he wrote in his "Christus":

> Oh, there is something in that voice that reaches
> The innermost recesses of my spirit.

His voice transcends the gulf of time to reach the minds of men in every generation.

Jesus said to His Disciples, "The shepherd . . . calleth his own sheep by name . . . and the sheep follow him: for they know his voice." His voice was not to be stilled by His death. Men and women of the Twentieth Century were to know the joy of hearing the voice of the Master.

Every consistent reader of the Gospels gives the Master a voice when he reads the words which Jesus spoke so many centuries ago. We humans clothe our God in a form which has some basis of physical reality. We see Jesus in a picture, or in a human form which best expresses what we have known Him to be. In a similar manner we give a voice to the Master. His words come to life as spoken by a familiar voice. It may be a mother's, or a father's voice which first uttered the words at a family altar. It may be a preacher's voice which brought into living reality for the first time the majesty of His holy life. But it will not be the voice of the Master until it seems with every phrase to answer the longings of the heart, and speak words of encouragement, or challenge. The voice of the Master always touches the depths of need.

We have no recording of the voice of the Master which can be amplified on any occasion to satisfy the taste of the listener. Perhaps it is as well that such a miracle is not available. Too easy an access to the voice of Jesus might close the ears of His followers to the endless spiritual sound waves which have carried His words across the centuries. Emanating from the Bible, they take on reality for those who have caught the secret of how to give a voice to the written word.

II

Consideration of the voice of the Master suggests several conclusions about the use of the voices of His followers.

First, a study of His voice gives emphasis to the wisdom of silence. Almost as impressive as His glorious teachings are the words which Jesus left unsaid. There are no fruitless phrases in the Gospels. Each word which He spoke seemed uttered for a special purpose.

At the trial and crucifixion His solitary grandeur stands out in greater majesty because He did not rail against His accusers. We read that, in response to their accusations, "He uttered not a word." It was the silence of Jesus which made the deeds of those who destroyed Him seem even more horrible.

Men in our generation tend to talk too much. Words are hurled at the average citizen from every hand. As if inspired by the abundant shower of words from the radio, the screen, and the newspaper, the virtue of silence has been forgotten.

There is an old Arab saying which reads: "You

are the master of the unspoken word: the spoken word is master of you." Silence is a mighty weapon for those whom anger, or fear, or hate would consume. A study of Jesus' life challenges His followers to cultivate the unspoken word.

Second, the use which the Master made of His voice demonstrates how the voice is expressive of the inner life. What Jesus said and how He said it reflected what He was.

A study of the art of public speaking is one of the hobbies which holds a fascination for many Americans. The desire to speak well in public is one phase of the fundamental human drive for social recognition. Many of those who teach voice cultivation center their efforts upon the expression of words and phrases. One such teacher gave her pupils a week's assignment to recite fifty times a day these words:

> My Mary's asleep by the murmuring stream.
> Most men want more money.

The late Professor Edmund C. Neil of Boston University, a very successful teacher of voice cultivation, approached the problem in an entirely different manner. He never gave his pupils an example of how a phrase should be spoken. He seldom asked a student to recite mere sentences. He labored to have the voice express inner thoughts and ideas. He argued that if the idea of a mountain becomes sufficiently conceived within the mind, then the voice will take on breadth and height sufficient to describe the mountain. It was his opinion that the voice is the perfect instrument to express the thoughts or ideas which govern the life of an individual.

Those who would attain the depth of feeling in the voice of the Master must cultivate the love for God and God's people that was in Jesus. Those who would have a voice which has the same quality of tenderness must cultivate His tenderness toward little children and the sick. Those who would have the voice of the Master which rang with indignation must be fired by righteous indignation against the evils of the world. The voice can become a perfect reflection of the inner life.

Third, we learn from the Master the power of words of encouragement. Petty criticisms tighten the vocal chords, and tend to make the voice smaller. Continued argument creates a voice which is high-pitched and shrill. But words of encouragement and comfort broaden and deepen the quality of the spoken word.

The power of the human voice to encourage and inspire men is unlimited. History has many pages which glow with the stories of those who have been lifted from the depths of despair by means of a few timely words.

Dr. Frederic Loomis, one of America's great

physicians, tells of an hour in Alaska when three brief sentences changed the course of his life. After completing one year of medical studies he was forced to leave school because of insufficient funds. He went to Alaska in the hope of making an easy fortune. Ten years went by and he never returned home to complete his medical training. One night two strangers came to share his cabin on their way back to the United States. They were present when a man who had been injured by an explosion came to him for assistance. They watched him, because no doctor was near, skillfully operate on the man's eyes. The following morning, when they were leaving, one of the men said: "Speaking tactfully as one gentleman to another, are you going to stay here hammering rock all your life? How long does it take you to get some sense? Or are you one of those who just don't care?" With that, they went away. But the voice came back again and again to Frederic Loomis. It made him uncomfortable. It left him dissatisfied with himself. And finally it drove him back to medical school, and to a splendid life of service.

The human voice is a precious instrument loaned by God to His children. Used unwisely it can become as colorless as a soul that has gone to sleep. But used to impart courage and faith, it takes on a beauty and strength which can transform life.

When Jesus spoke those who heard Him listened breathlessly! His voice was not silenced in death. The Gospel of John quotes the Master as saying: "Everyone that is of the truth heareth my voice." So today that voice is lifted against the entrenched evil and suffering which surround us. In great churches, and in the solitude of the smallest home, we are privileged to hear the voice of the Master.

CHAPTER IX

The Name of the Master

Text: "Wherefore God highly exalted Him; and gave Him a name that is above every name; that in the name of Jesus every knee should bow." — *Philippians 2: 9*

HEBREW boys were often named "Jesus" in the centuries before the birth of Christ. It was a popular name among those who looked back with pride to the history of their nation. In the Hebrew language the name was Joshua, meaning "Jehovah is Salvation." Parents were proud to call their sons after the strong man who took up the mantle of leadership upon the death of Moses.

In the decades following the birth of the Reformation the name of Jesus became so revered that, as Protestant parents would not give their sons the name of Jehovah, so they would not use the human name of the Christ. It was "a name that is above every name."

I

The coming of a newborn babe to a home often provokes long discussions as to what it shall be called.

Sometimes the child is named after the mother or the father, or a greatly admired relative. Any adult is honored by a child who bears his name.

Many of our common names have an origin which should inspire noble endeavors. When a child is called "Grace" she is blessed with a name of great honor. She must always be challenged to show "love for others, not according to their worthiness, but according to their needs." A boy named Ernest is pledged to face responsibility with earnestness. Hiram has been honored with the title, "Most noble." A child given the name of Elizabeth is forever "consecrated to God"; Dorothy is "a gift of God." These are names with a verbal origin in which the parents have expressed a hope that their child's life will be a worthy one.

Another group of names has been chosen again and again because of great lives associated with them. More girls are called "Mary" than by any other name; and the reason is plain. The mother of Jesus has remained the perfect example of motherhood. Ruth is a common name for girls. The recollection of the loyalty and love in the life of the first Ruth gives honor to the name. Boys called "Paul," or "John," or "James" have a great responsibility to live up to the example of the men who played such a great part in the early spread of the Christian faith.

Yet parents seldom name their children Jesus!

[101]

And why? Because it is "a name that is above every name." In the American way of life the highest honor which can be bestowed on a citizen is to be elected the President of the United States. A boy child is sometimes called George, and the parents hope he may be like George Washington; or he is named Thomas, and there is an unexpressed desire that he may grow to be a second Thomas Jefferson. But no baby is named Jesus! Associated with that name there is a Divine Presence which even the dreaming heart of a mother cannot conceive as being the lot of her child.

The name of Jesus does not lose its meaning and power with a change of language. It has the same fascination for people in every part of the world. A. Hamilton Gibbs wrote a book in which his leading character made an intense search for happiness. While on the quest he lived in different countries. In order to learn whether the people had the peace of mind for which he sought, he lived as one of them. His name was John. When he resided in France as a Frenchman, he changed it to Jean; in Germany he became Johann; in Spain he was Giovanni.

The name of Jesus holds the same power over the lives of men in whatever language it is spoken. The seeker for peace does not need to hurry away to a foreign country to carry on his search. The name of Jesus in any language satisfies the restless spirit of man.

This generation has lived in the shadow of big personalities. Hitler and Mussolini were names which once struck terror in the human heart. The names of Churchill, Roosevelt, and Stalin were often on human lips. In those names men recognized a power to change the life of the world.

But there is a name which truly changes life. It is the name of Jesus. Paul reminds the followers of Christ that "God highly exalted Him; and gave Him a name that is above every name; that in the name of Jesus every knee should bow." It was in the spirit of that verse that Lydia Baxter wrote the words of the familiar hymn:

Take the Name of Jesus with you,
    Child of sorrow and of woe;
It will joy and comfort give you —
    Take it, then, where'er you go.

Take the Name of Jesus ever,
    As a shield from every snare;
If temptations round you gather,
    Breathe that holy Name in prayer.

The biggest names in history have diminished in influence with the passing centuries. It is said that mothers in various parts of Europe once would frighten their children into doing what was right by saying, "Napoleon will get you!" And adults as well knew the terror of that name. Yet Napoleon has become little more than a page in the books of history. The name of Alexander the Great struck a similar terror in men's lives. But he, too, occupies an obscure place in the panorama of history.

The name of Jesus, however, grows in meaning and influence with the passing centuries. Many portions of the world which had not heard His name one hundred years ago now build churches and chapels to His honor. Beginning in an obscure province of the mighty Roman Empire twenty centuries ago, Jesus has marched onward into the life of the world, and into the hearts of men.

II

People the world over are looking for a name. "Give us a Name!" they cry. "We must have a Name!"

1. They grope for a Name that can heal the wounds of a broken world. In recent years a new consciousness has been born in the mind of man that all is not well with what we know as "civilization." Two wars of world proportion, with an economic disaster sandwiched between, have shaken all the confidence which had been generated through an amazing century of inventive miracles.

As the feeling of security has been undermined, men have looked for a Name which can answer the needs of the hour. The people of Italy once were certain that they had the answer in Mussolini and his Fascism; the people of Germany were sure their answer was in the name of Hitler. Vast numbers of intellectuals in Europe shouted the name of Frederick Nietzsche as the prophet of a necessary road to power. Millions of others bowed before the name of Karl Marx as the herald of the new day.

Jesus of Nazareth was not an economist. He did not live in a day when the world could be circled in an instant by the miracle of radio, and in which men could be transported from one portion of the globe to another by the wonder of the airplane. His was a slow-moving civilization with comparatively simple economic needs.

Yet Jesus knew human nature! And knowing the needs of men, He was able to present to His followers the teachings and goals which He deemed necessary for those whom He honored with the title, "Children of God." Those teachings and goals have proved strangely effective in the changing world. The growing civilization of Europe in the tenth and eleventh centuries climbed to greatness on the wings of faith in the Christian Gospel. England of the Wesleyan era was saved from an inner chaos more dangerous than a foreign invasion by a new discovery of the power of Christianity. The vast expansion of the United States to the Pacific Coast in the Nineteenth Century attained a rare height of human achievement by reason of the

Christian faith which inspired so many of the builders of that new world. Again and again the name of the Master has been sufficient for the changing human scene.

No part of the world has ever tried in their entirety the teachings of Christ. What He had to say concerning man's responsibility to God, and to his neighbor, still seems visionary. But the world has ceased to prosper under other leadership. The pressing situation cries desperately for a leader who can point the pathway out of the vale of tears and suffering. The hour has come when the teachings of Christ must be considered more seriously than ever before by our tottering civilization.

With eager eyes men gaze into the distance, hoping to see a banner which will tell the name of a man to lead the way out of chaos. Such a banner the Christian Church proudly waves before the warring world! And on it is a name! The name of Jesus! The Apostle Paul wrote to the people of a city which was desperately needing help: "Wherefore God highly exalted Him; and gave Him a name that is above every name; that in the name of Jesus every knee should bow." A new day of hope for the world will dawn when men kneel on bended knee before the name of the Master.

2. Men are groping also for a name which can answer the widespread doubts concerning God. The

desire to know the Eternal Builder of the Universe is as deep in the human heart as is life itself. There is no health for men who breathe continually the air of doubt. Faith in God is as necessary to victorious living as is food and shelter. Men can never be at peace until they have found their proper relationship to the Creator.

The anxiety of the human heart to know God is poignantly expressed in the words of Amos N. Wilder:

> I have a heart that cries to God
> Abandonedly across the blind
> Imperfect avenue of mind,
> I have a heart that cries to God.
> I have a heart that cries to God
> Across the quarried stones of thought,
> The labored temple slowly wrought,
> A heart, a heart that cries to God.
> I have a heart that cries to God
> Immediately and must dispense
> With faltering through the world of sense,
> And calls across the mind to God;
> That calls across the worlds to God,
> Nor stays to elaborate the tongue
> Of sacrament too slowly wrung,
> I have a heart that cries to God.

Men who grope for truth about God have often found the clearest road to His feet in the revelation of Christ. It remains a mystery how the seeker may look into the face of Jesus, and suddenly warm to the assurance that God is like Him. But the strange event has been repeated on millions of occasions. The name of the Master does usher men into the Presence of God.

Dr. Frederic Loomis, a great American physician, tells of a Christmas Eve when God became very real to him. He had returned home at midnight after completing a hectic round of professional services. He arrived completely exhausted and cold. As if his other burdens were not sufficient, he found that the furnace fire had gone out. It was necessary to go to the cellar, and work for an hour building another fire. At last the task was completed. He climbed the stairs wearily to his room and, still shivering from the intense cold, he prepared for bed. Just as he slipped under the covers the telephone rang. It was the hospital calling to inform him of an emergency case which demanded his immediate attention. Then it was that the reserve of human endurance broke down. He raged in anger against a godless world and a pitiless fate. While still he shouted his doubt and anger he heard a child's voice lifted in song. His tiny two-year-old daughter was standing at the foot of her crib in the next room, and was singing the Christmas carol which her mother had prepared as a surprise for him. The tiny voice pierced through his gloom. Then the words she sang took on new meaning:

Silent night, Holy night,
All is calm, all is bright;

. . . .

Jesus, Lord, at Thy Birth.

The name of the Master performed the same miracle that night which has occurred on countless other occasions. The doctor's anger ceased, his doubts concerning the justice of life disappeared. There stole within his wearied spirit the reminder that God had not forgotten His people.

There are men and women in every corner of the world who have drifted far from the Presence of God. The cruelty of an unjust fate looms before them as the largest factor in their lives. For them there is no child to sing, at the moment of greatest need, the reminder that God made Himself known through the life of Jesus of Nazareth. Yet for all such men there is a name which can turn away the spears of doubt. It is the name of Jesus!

3. Men also grope for the Name which can give meaning to life. There is nothing which contributes so much to despair as the discovery that there is no purpose in all our human striving.

A Seeker for Truth one day awoke in a fog of loneliness, and determined to search for the Castle of Human Dreams in which he hoped to find life's true Meaning and Purpose. Someone told the Seeker that there was only one road to the Castle, and that was the Way of Pleasure. With eager step he hurried down that way. At first he was not weary. There were many others on the path, and laughter and dancing filled every hour of the day. Sometimes the Seeker forgot the Castle of Human Dreams in the hurry and the gaiety. But at last his step grew uncertain, and weariness made the mad laughter of those about him seem an empty thing. The longing returned to reach his goal. When the Seeker expressed his doubts to the Ruler of the Road, he was greeted with laughter. "Be not concerned!" he cried. "Enjoy thy life." But the hunger for something more than Pleasure had gripped his soul. "Tell me," he insisted, "has anyone ever reached the Castle of Human Dreams by following this road?" The Ruler of the Way of Pleasure halted. "Well, no, not exactly," he answered soberly. Then his smile returned. "But come on," he shouted, "we're on the way!"

Then the Seeker knew that the Road of Pleasure had led him astray. Another voyager, seeing his hesitation, asked him if he had tried the Way of Material Gain. He assured the Traveller that the Castle he sought was at the end of that road. Again the Seeker plunged onward with eager step. He had much company on the way. As his mad efforts earned additional rewards of gold the travellers grew fewer. At last he was almost alone. His load of wealth became oppressive. He all but stumbled and fell under the weight of it. It was then he met the Ruler of the Road of Material Gain. "Is the Castle of Dreams far away?" the Seeker anxiously asked. Without giving him an answer the Ruler examined his pack of gold. "It's a wonderful pack," he said. "But is the Castle close by?" insisted the Seeker. The Ruler hesitated. "I do not know," he answered. "I have never seen it; but with all your Pack of Gold, your Castle of Dreams must be close by." Then the Seeker knew that all the striving had been in vain. The Road of Material Gain was lined with great houses wherein were physical satisfactions, but it did not lead to the Castle of Human Dreams.

As the Seeker sat by the roadside and wept bitter tears, he was aware of two young men on a narrow path not far away. Their faces were bright with something he had not seen in many days. They seemed more to run than to walk, and yet they were not weary. The Seeker called out to them, "What is the name of the road you are travelling? And where does it go?" The young men halted at the sound of his voice. "This is the road which Jesus walked," they answered. "Its name is the Jesus' Way. It leads to the Kingdom." The Seeker, now grown old, unsteadily arose. "Is the Castle of Human Dreams far away?" he asked. "Oh, no!" came the quick answer. "The Castle of Human Dreams is yonder! So is the House of Hope; and the Mansion of Comfort!" The old man laid aside his pack of gold, and joined the youths on the Way of Jesus. As he walked onward he saw that other travellers were like the youths. Their step was quick and sure; their laughter was the joy of new discovery. Even as he travelled with them he felt the burden of his years fall away. He, too, was a youth again. Then in the distance he saw the Castle of Human Dreams. The Way of Jesus had brought him home.

III

Men today are anxiously looking for a Name; a name that can open the window of the soul to the Presence of God; a name which can heal the hurts of the broken world; a name that can give meaning and purpose to all of living. The name of the Master satisfies all those needs. The poet proclaimed the last best hope of man in these words:

> I know a life that is lost to God,
>   Bowed down by the things of earth;
> But I know a Name! a Name! a Name!
>   That can bring that soul new birth.

It is the name of Jesus!

CHAPTER X

The Marks of the Master

Text: "I bear in my body the marks of the Lord Jesus."
— *Galatians 6: 17*

THE Apostle Paul always wrote with pride concerning the hardships which he suffered while preaching the Gospel of Christ. In his letter to the Galatians he reminded his readers that in one of their cities he was stoned, and left for dead. In another he was lashed. In a third he was thrown into prison and shackled to the wall of a dungeon cell. It was the remembrance of those sufferings which led him to say, proudly: "I bear in my body the marks of the Lord Jesus."

By the end of the First Century Christians were regarding the marks of the Master in a different manner. When they spoke of "the marks of Jesus" they referred to the nailprints in Jesus' hands and feet, and the scar indicating where the spear was thrust into His side. It became the noblest hope of a faithful Christian to live so devoutly as to receive the same marks in his own body.

Many of the followers of St. Francis of Assisi declared that he had these "stigmata." The claim for such a phenomenon was made no more than two years after his death by Thomas de Celano, the biographer appointed by Pope Gregory IX. He wrote that, after long meditation and prayer on the fact of the crucifixion, "St. Francis' hands and feet appeared transfixed in the middle with nails; the head of the nails appearing on the inner side of the hands, and on the upper side of the feet, while the points were on the other side. . . . His right side was as if transfixed by a spear."

A similar manifestation of faithfulness was claimed for Catherine of Siena by her followers. Her "stigmata" were described as being clearly evident after a Communion Service during which she had prayed long and devoutly that she might be worthy of the suffering of Christ.

Whether or not there is reason to accept the truth of these recorded experiences of faithful Christians of centuries past, it is certain that there is no expectation that such a miracle will be repeated in the life of the Christian today. Men do not look for nailprints or spear scars. Nor do they expect that many of His followers will bear with Paul the marks of stonings, or beatings, or long imprisonment. Yet no Christian can escape the challenge of Paul's words. Every follower of the Man of Nazareth should be able to say, "I bear in my body the marks of the Lord Jesus."

I

What marks of the Master should be evident in the bodies of His followers today? First, the Christian ought to have Calloused Knees from hours spent in prayer. A government official recently challenged the American people to "harden your hands with toil until the callouses stand out, and become your medals of honor." Hardened hands tell eloquently of hours spent with tools and machines. The faithful Christian will be worthy of greater honor when the callouses are not only on his hands, but on his knees as well. Such marks tell of hours spent in the Presence of God.

The fact that Jesus prayed is emphasized many times in the Gospel narratives. It mattered not how weary He was after the work of the day, He found time for prayer. Indeed, the greater the drain became upon His personal strength, the more time He spent in conversations with His Heavenly Father. When the threat against His personal safety seemed to justify bold action, He answered the challenge with more hours spent in prayer.

It is impossible to think steadily of the Master without picturing Him on His knees. The Hoffman portrait of "Christ in Gethsemane" is popular, not only because the face reflects what millions expect to find in the face of Christ, but because it shows the Master on His knees in prayer. It is on His knees that His followers know Him best.

As it is impossible to separate Jesus from the act of prayer, so it should be in the life of the faithful follower of the Master. Calloused knees are the mark of faithfulness which should be in evidence in the body of every Christian.

The need for a return to a prayer-centered faith has become a major emphasis in both the pulpit and the religious press in our day. Leaders of Christian thought have impressed Church leaders with the close connection which prevails between an active prayer life and the hope for a better world. Psychiatrists and other men of science have expressed an interest in personal religious devotion. That was made clear by Dr. Alexis Carrel in a memorable article on the subject of "Prayer."

"Today, as never before," he said, "prayer is a binding necessity in the lives of men and nations. The lack of emphasis upon the religious sense has brought the world to the edge of destruction. Our deepest source of power and perfection has been left miserably undeveloped. Prayer, the basic exercise of the spirit, must be actively practised in our private lives. The neglected soul of man must be made strong enough to assert itself once more. For if the power of prayer is again released and used in the lives of common men and women; if the spirit declares its aims clearly and boldly, there is yet hope that our prayer for a better world will be answered."

Prayer is one of the weapons by which Christians may help to forge a better world. Recognizing that fact, the true follower of Christ will bear in his body the marks of Jesus — Calloused Knees — from hours spent in prayer.

II

In the second place, the modern marks of the Master are Tired Hands and Weary Feet. Jesus' life was devoted to the service of others. The dawn of many of the days reported in the Gospels found Jesus already at work with the task of ministering to the needy. As the sun climbed high in the heavens, and beat down with the scorching heat of noonday, He was still busy with the ministry of service. When the setting sun had left the Western horizon and darkness had laid a cloud over the land, even then the Master might have been seen in the firelight laboring for those in need. The life of Jesus was marked by Tired Hands and Weary Feet.

The compelling need for service is inescapable for any Christian who has caught the spirit of the Master. There can be no hesitation or postponement of obligations to do His will. Men gain strength in hours of dark despair through the irrepressible human hope that tomorrow will bring relief from pain. But the hope of a better world is not alone a cause for satisfaction. It is an urgent call to action as well.

Miss Maud Slye is one of the noblest spirits of

this century. Her dramatic story is told by B. L. Jaffe in his "Outposts of Science." In 1898, as a young college graduate, Miss Slye began a study of the habits and diseases of mice. She was interested in the insight which such a study might give into the diseases of mankind. Before five years had passed she was caring for more than two thousand of the tiny creatures. In 1910 she discovered that mice are strangely subject to cancer germs. Such a condition made them excellent objects for the study of the origin and possible cure of the disease. Five years later there were more than 10,000 caged mice in her laboratories. Through painstaking observation over weary months and years, she has made discoveries which offer the basis for the hope that mankind will finally conquer this dread disease. It was she who found that cancer tends to be hereditary. She later demonstrated that the disease often develops at a place of irritation. In 1918, a thunderstorm in the night sent her hurrying to the laboratory to make certain no harm had come to the mice. From then on she gave up her home, lived in the laboratory, and devoted her entire life to the care and study of the little creatures so important to her experiments. Always before her there was a hope that she might play a part in the final conquest of disease. Miss Slye wrote a poem of service which is eloquent of her own life. The last two lines are as follows:

It was for me to know the tired hands, the weary feet,
But oh! the joy within my heart.

In a less spectacular, but no less urgent form, the call of service is offered to every follower of the Master of Men. Every Christian should have moments when he can say, " I bear in my body the marks of the Lord Jesus — Tired Hands and Weary Feet."

III

The cry of pain from suffering humanity calls for another mark of the Master — Cheeks Wet with Tears of Sympathy. The unfailing compassion of Christ stands out in bold relief in the Gospel record. The lepers, the blind, and the bereaved all received, not only help, but a personal interest which was born of sympathy. Jesus suffered with those who were bearing pain or sorrow.

The anguish of our world is appalling beyond that of any generation in recorded history. Some measure of the suffering of national groups in Europe has become clearer to the American people. We gain from time to time a slight conception of what it means for millions of women and children to be hungry and homeless. Yet the world's suffering is so widespread that people far removed from the scene of action tend to become hardened to it. Millions of Americans laughed at a Hollywood comedy which made sport of the destruction of Warsaw.

If the hour ever strikes when the hearts of Christians fail to respond sympathetically to the presence of cruelty and suffering, that hour will mark the beginning of a new spiritual darkness in the world. There is reason to hope, however, that this will not happen. Thousands of Christians today are bearing in their bodies the mark of the Lord Jesus — Cheeks Wet with Tears of Sympathy.

Robert St. John related a deeply moving experience of the time when, with other newspapermen, he was fleeing from Yugoslavia before the advancing enemy. They had arrived at Sarajevo. Suddenly the bombers came! They dropped their cargoes of destruction on every side. Mr. St. John and his friends decided that they must dash through the town to the safety of the hills beyond. Nothing must be allowed to halt their mad flight. They knew that it was only through haste that they could hope to survive. In a few moments they were on their way! The car careened back and forth among the ruins. But at last they were forced by the very destruction about them to go more slowly. Very slowly. As they edged near the curb in a narrow street they heard a cry of pain. On the sidewalk lay a bloody and broken hulk of humanity. Mr. St. John halted the car, and climbed out to kneel beside the wounded man. One of his companions shouted in protest. Without pausing to answer him, Mr. St. John picked up the victim of the bombing. There were curses from the back seat. "Put him down! Can't you see he is nearly dead?" They were right. The man was dying. But the cry of lonely pain had called into action all of Mr. St. John's reserves of sympathy. He could not leave the man to suffer alone. He laid him tenderly on the floor of the car. Then he drove on to where stretcher bearers were searching among the ruins for victims. He left the man in their care. Valuable time had been lost, but for Mr. St. John a life-long dream had been kept alive. He could still hope for a better world in the years ahead when men will share each other's anguish.

Out of the chaotic experiences of this generation a new World will be born. Whether it will be better than the world which preceded it is still an unanswered question. But it will be more tragic and pitiable if Christians become so hard of heart that we fail to reach out a hand in sympathy whenever humanity cries out in pain.

IV

Paul sealed his letter to the Galatian Churches with the proud assertion, "I bear in my body the marks of the Lord Jesus." We who call ourselves Christians in this generation are summoned to seal our proclamation of faith with a similar declaration. Our marks will differ from those borne by St. Paul. But one fact is certain! We will carry with us the marks of the Master.

CHAPTER XI

The Look of the Master

Text: "And Jesus, looking on him, loved him." — *Mark 10: 21*

THE "look" of a man is as much a part of his real self as are his hands or feet. The brief records which are usually assembled to identify a person — the color of his eyes and hair, his height, weight, and age — these serve to mark him as different from his fellows for people who deal in statistics. But they fail to tell much which reveals his true worth of character. Intangibles become significant when we try to understand what a man really is. Among the indefinite qualities by which the character may be judged there is the "look" of a man.

I talked one day to a highly-skilled oculist. I spoke of the satisfaction which he must feel in being able so directly to serve others. They came into his office, I said, with vision impaired, and went out able to look on the world with new eyes. "True," he answered, "I am able to assist people. Yet let me tell you the discouraging side of my professional work. I improve the vision of those whose eyes have been ruined by steady concentration on trivial things. And after the vision is corrected I know that the eyes will not be used for anything worth the seeing. I can't control what they look at!" The doctor was saying that the "look" of a man is important.

A motion picture star was recently engaged to play the leading part in a feature in technicolor. On the very day when the picture was to begin it was discovered that the star had blue eyes. But blue eyes will not photograph in color. There was a hurried consultation with Theodore Obrig, the famed optician, who specializes in making contact lenses. At tremendous expense the star was fitted to lenses which changed the color of her eyes from blue to brown, and which enabled the picture to continue. After all the publicity and effort we might expect that the eyes would look on something important, or share in a plot which had significance. But no! The eyes, changed in color by such great effort, merely gazed languidly on the sensual and material portion of the world.

We know far more about "the look of the Master" than we do about any of His physical characteristics. The color of His eyes must remain forever a mystery. His height, weight, and features are beyond our power to describe. But we are given a picture on many occasions in the Gospels of "the look of the Master." We know what Jesus looked upon, and in those glimpses we see Him as He really was.

The gaze of Jesus was not fixed continually on
things ethereal. He stooped often to look into the
places of human need. Frederick Langbridge wrote
a poem containing two lines which summarize widely
divergent philosophies of life:

> Two men looked through the self-same bars;
> One saw mud; the other saw stars.

The man who saw "stars" must not be thought of
as "starry-eyed." Mr. Langbridge meant that the man
of vision looked upon the ugly and uncouth, but then
saw something beyond the outward appearance that
was worth the remembering. It was so with Jesus.
He gazed upon the same situations and people con-
fronting others. They saw only mud, while He saw
stars!

The "look of the Master" becomes unmistakable
early in the Gospel record of His ministry. In the
account of the Temptation He is taken to the summit
of a high mountain. The writer of the Gospel says
that "the devil showed Him all the Kingdoms of the
world." His guide expected that He would see the
wealth and opportunities of power spread out before
Him. But the Master saw further than the material
glory of the world. His gaze reached beyond the
armed might of the world's soldiers, the mighty
buildings of stone, and the statues of gold. His "look"

pierced through the gaudy exterior of things to where lay the wistful longings of humanity.

It is as easy today as it was in the time of the Master for the outlook of man to end with armed might or material power. The tear-stained cheeks of suffering women and children are easily forgotten in the glory of a victorious army marching into an enemy city. The sight of silver bombers bearing the insignia of our country, and carrying a load of death against an enemy city, becomes a picture of beauty. It is only men with the "look of the Master" who see the human tragedy of bombings which are borne more by the helpless than by the strong.

In his "Letter from New Guinea" Vern Haugland related one of the finest tales of individual courage which came out of the days of war. After having parachuted from a bomber into the jungles of New Guinea, the young newspaperman wandered for forty-two days in the mountainous wilds. Without food, and in constant danger, his growing faith in God was a solemn challenge to men of lesser faith. After the forty-two days of wandering he discovered a native village. He found the people sympathetic, and eager to help the stranger. He saw them as human beings with like feelings to his own. He responded to friendliness with friendliness; to comradeship with comradeship. As he looked upon them he saw what was admirable in their simple manner of living. He was perplexed several days later when he was carried by the natives to another village where there were white men. There he found the white men treated the natives as if they were inhuman, and acted the part of white overlords.

Mr. Haugland and the other white men saw the same natives. They observed the same habits, and the same personalities. But Mr. Haugland looked on them with the "look of the Master." The others observed what Jesus was expected to see from the top of the Mount of Temptation. They saw the black men as loot to be plundered. The American newspaperman saw them as human beings who could be kind, and deserved kindness in return.

Both professional and amateur physicians are prescribing remedies for our sick world. The cures range far and wide over the economic, sociological, and psychological programs known to men. Many of the programs would, if they were put into practise, go far toward curing the patient of his illness. But nothing promises a more certain cure for the ills of both individuals and nations than a widespread cultivation of the "look of the Master."

II

Three incidents in the Gospel record reveal the way in which the eyes of Jesus sought out and challenged the individual.

First, there is the look which He gave to youth.

When the Master met the rich young ruler we read that " Jesus, looking on him, loved him."

In commenting upon this verse the prophetic voices across the ages have concentrated largely on the word " rich." It was his wealth and position which drew their interest. There is equal reason in the passage to center the thought on the word " youth." Here was a young man. His whole life lay before him. The Master saw his possibilities as a youth. He recognized the importance of his wealth and position, but their importance lay in the fact that they might be used in a lifetime of service.

The " look " of the Master was always centered on youth. The comparatively brief portraits which the Gospels give us of His ministry reveal many instances when He was concerned with young people. The tenderest fellowship in the inner group of Twelve Disciples was reserved for the young man, John.

In the centuries since the time of Christ it is young people who have most often felt the relentless challenge of the " look " of the Master. William Wilberforce had such an experience. As a young man of twenty-one he was elected to the British Parliament. His first years in London were spent in seeking for pleasure. He became celebrated as a gambler. After two years of carefree life he went to Northern England for a holiday with Isaac Miller, a boyhood friend and companion. Together they read aloud the New

Testament in Greek. Throughout those days he said that he seemed to feel unseen eyes fixed upon him. Later, when he returned to London, the old way of life became unbearable. He wrote: "I must awake to my dangerous state, and never be at rest until I have made my peace with God." William Wilberforce had experienced the challenge of "the look of the Master."

Such has often been the experience of young men. Augustine, John Wesley, Francis of Assisi, and innumerable others knew in their youth the breathless moment which came to the rich young ruler when "Jesus, looking on him, loved him."

The divine concern for the youth of the world has not now come to an end. Young people, before whom the door to life's great opportunity is about to open, are still sought by the Master of Men. His "look" still probes beneath the air of bored sophistication which youth often cultivates to avoid the responsibility of answering the challenge to higher things. No youth of our day will reach the goal worthy of his best self until he has the same experience which came to the rich young ruler when "Jesus, looking on him, loved him."

Second, there is the look which Jesus gave to the people in need. The writer of the Gospel tells us that "He saw Peter's wife's mother, lying sick of the fever." The incident occurred at the close of a busy day in the life of the Master. He had poured out His energies unsparingly. All through the day He had toiled to heal the sick of body and mind. It was now night. By all the rules of humanity He was entitled to think of His work as completed. He had earned His rest. But the narrative tells us that "He saw Peter's wife's mother." Hardly had Jesus and His Disciples entered the humble home when "the look of the Master" came to rest upon the only place in the home where there was misery and pain.

Even a casual study of the Scriptures reveals the unmistakable truth that Jesus responded to human need and suffering at every point of contact. His "look" was always peering under the surface, or beyond the crowd to someone in pain, or hardship, or loneliness.

If the personal interest of Jesus in the needs of people had ended with His earthly life, then it would suffice to comment here upon a remarkable human personality and example. But it is more than that. The Master is the reflection of the Creator God. His concern for human need mirrors the eternal concern of the Father God for the lives of His children. It is that fact which hosts of Christians have discovered for themselves. As Jesus "saw Peter's wife's mother, lying sick of the fever," so God sees the Peters of our day, and their wives, and their mothers. No human tragedy falls beyond the reach of the divine care.

The "look" of the Master encompasses human need wherever it is found. It is a look which has an abundance of sympathy and understanding.

Third, there is the look which Jesus gave to the people whom the world passes by or, if it deigns to notice them at all, is satisfied to dismiss as insignificant. Jesus often paused to recognize such persons. Others might speak with disregard of the " common people " but, for the Master, there were no " common men."

Look at Him on a day when He walked down the Galilean road. Into the narrative is interjected the words: "As Jesus passed by, He saw a man." He wasn't much of a man by the world's standards. His position as a taxgatherer relegated him to a place among the outcasts. His job was not only humble, but was in the service of the invader. No self-respecting person would associate with him. But Jesus saw something in the man which others did not consider. His "look" pierced beyond the rough exterior and the despised vocation to the haunting dreams which set his heart beating faster with hope. Before their conversation was finished the man was numbered with the Disciples of Jesus. His name was Matthew.

Such has always been the way of the Master. He was always seeing "a man" or "a woman" where others could only see a passing crowd.

Muretus, an eminent French scholar of the Eighteenth Century, was taken suddenly ill while travelling in remote Lombardy. His fame was unknown to anyone in that portion of France. When he was picked up unconscious on the road, and no one could tell who he was, he was carried to a pauper hospital. In the days that followed he was close to death. When he returned from the land of the unconscious he heard two physicians discussing his case as they stood by his bed. One of them said in Latin: "*Faciamus experimentum anima vili.*" "Let us make an experiment with this vile creature." Muretus astounded them by answering in Latin: "*Vilum animum appelas pro qua Christus dedignatus est morti.*" Translated, he was saying, "Will you call anyone worthless for whom Christ died?"

A reminder of the worth of human personality has been needed in every age of the world's history. Those who have caught the spirit of the Master have known that His love, and concern, and sacrifice reached out to them. His way of seeing possibilities for greatness in the lives of the humblest of men has lifted whole countries and continents from their foundations. When men of power have failed to keep the glow of service in their lives, and have sold out to the god of material satisfactions, the Master has always raised some humble man to where he caught a new vision of his powers and responsibilities.

Miss Salimen's "Katrina" is one of the finest books

written in this century. She tells the story of a girl who lived in the Aland Islands off the coast of Sweden. Katrina refused many offers of marriage from the young men of the fishing village which was her home. She dreamed of a hero who would come like a knight of olden days to claim his fair lady. One day the hero appeared. He came on a fishing boat which stopped in the tiny harbor near her village for security in a storm. When Katrina saw Johan with his tall, straight body and wavy hair she knew immediately that this was the man for whom she had been waiting. It was not long until Johan was telling her of his love. He told her of the mansion in which he lived at home, and of his wealth. It seemed to Katrina that her dreams had been completely fulfilled. And so they were married! Then Johan took her to his island home. When they went ashore she looked in vain for the promised mansion on the hill. She could see no signs of wealth and luxury. She turned to Johan with puzzled eyes which pleaded for an explanation. Johan's hour of confession had come. He admitted to her that his tales of wealth and position were lies. He had no money. He led her to the one-room shack which was his only home. It was bare of all furnishings except a box and a rudely made bed.

Many women would have cried out in despair and anger against the cruel deceit. Katrina said not a word. She set about making a home out of the ugly shack.

She had married an indolent deceiver, but she saw qualities in him which even he did not know he possessed. She developed him, led him on, and slowly wrought a manly character.

It was that way with the Master of Men. He always saw the hidden good beyond the outward evil. He always sensed the unexpressed longings beyond the masked attitude of indifference. No matter how many times the dreams of godliness had been forgotten in lies, deceit, and greed, He still saw the person who might be born out of the ruin of a life.

The "look" of the Master is one that sees the far reaches of human hope. What men have been is important; what men may be is of greater importance. Every wanderer on the road of life, and every Christian as well, stands clearly defined before His steady eyes. But it is not a look of condemnation, nor of scorn. It is a look which is filled with love, and a saving power from every evil. In it there is a wistful sense of what life can become. The "look" of the Master sees beyond the mud to the stars!

CHAPTER XII

The Tears of the Master

Text: "Jesus wept." — *John 11: 35*

ANYONE who would understand human nature must take sorrow into consideration. It is one of the experiences common to all mankind. It was A. W. E. O'Shaughnessy who wrote:

> If you go over desert and mountain,
>   Far into the country of Sorrow,
>   Today and tonight and tomorrow,
>   And maybe for months and for years;
>   You shall come with a heart that is bursting
>   For trouble and toiling and thirsting,
>   You shall certainly come to the fountain
>   At length, — to the Fountain of Tears.

Joy is a part of man's heritage and life, but so is sorrow. Eyes often shine with delight, but the same eyes are as often bathed with tears.

The incidents in the Bible which report that Jesus shed tears have not always been welcomed by His followers. A weeping Lord does not fit appropriately into a conception of Jesus as King of Kings and Lord of Lords. Better forget the tears of the Master, they have said. Let the record be as silent concerning His tears as it is concerning His laughter. But the tears of the Master have left their mark on the pages of the Word of God. They cannot be blotted out or wiped away. They are a part of Himself. They give the eager seeker for truth a further insight into the mystery of the Divine Love as revealed in the life of Jesus Christ.

The tears of the Master are mentioned three times in the New Testament. The passages are less numerous than those dealing with other observable characteristics. Yet each reference adds its knowledge and inspiration to the seeker for truth.

I

The first tears of the Master were shed in sympathy for the sorrow of others. The Master was devoted to the family of Mary, and Martha, and Lazarus. His love for the home in which they lived in Bethany is altogether unique in the recorded experiences of His earthly life. He was at ease in the home of the Disciple Peter, but His fondness for the family of Lazarus went even deeper.

As Jesus labored near Jericho there came a messenger to tell Him that Lazarus was sick. When His work was completed, He took the road which led through Bethany to Jerusalem. Even before He came to the home of His friends the sad news was brought to Him that Lazarus was dead. In that hour Jesus wept. Some scholars have maintained that "Jesus wept" because He was about to call Lazarus back from the heavenly streets. But why look so far for a grief which was born of love? Jesus loved Lazarus. He loved the sisters who lived in the Bethany home. Their grief touched the depths of His spirit. He was ready to walk with them down through the valley of sorrow.

At some time during the first five centuries after Christ — but far removed from the physical life of Jesus — a scholar was dividing the Gospel of St. John into chapters and verses. What emotion must have stirred him when he came to the words, "Jesus wept." They were significant because they were expressive of Christ's sympathetic understanding of human sorrow. The scholar felt he must set them apart. What is the shortest verse in the Bible? Even stumbling Christians know the answer. It is the passage in St. John with only two short words set apart in a verse by themselves. They were for the scholar a pledge of divine love and sympathy.

There are other passages in the Gospels which picture Jesus as interested in the suffering of others. The sickness of a centurion's son, or the touch of a sick woman, or the cries of those who were blind brought an answering hand to help them. He was busy early and late in the work of ministering to the sick. But it remained for St. John to tell how the death of Lazarus affected Him personally. His concern for His friends not only called Him to action, but it called forth tears of sympathy.

The Christian who walks in the way of his Master will often be brought to tears as he shares the sorrows of friends and loved ones. The Spartan-like hardness which boasts that weeping is weakness has its place in life. But a life without tears of sympathy is bereft of depth and glory. Strong men marched over the European continent in this generation boasting that "Nordics do not weep; they make others weep." And life was an agony in the path where they walked.

The followers of Jesus of Nazareth will be strong in times of trial. But they will not forget the pain of others. Bayard Taylor was right when he said that "the bravest are the tenderest." The example of the Master is still the guide for those who bear His name.

One day death crept unannounced into a beautiful home and claimed the wife of a great Christian gentleman. He had a partner in business who lived four hundred miles away. They were more than business associates; they were partners in faith. They had been boys together in the same church, and had bowed at the same altar in recognition of the call to become followers of Jesus Christ. A telegram went to that friend telling of his partner's sorrow. No one could explain later how the friend arrived at the bereaved home so quickly. All the man knew was that he must be with his friend in the hour when he was sorrowing. I saw those big, strong men of the world as they met. Their hands clasped, and unspoken sympathy bound them together. Tears ran unchecked down the cheeks of the friend. The Christian friendship was sealed by love in that hour of sorrow.

Make no mistake about it, the tears of the Master are a summons to His followers to keep a spirit of sympathy so real a part of life that tears will flow when hearts are broken. T. B. Aldrich wrote:

> Dear Lord, though I be changed to senseless clay,
> And serve the Potter as he turns his wheel,
> I thank Thee for the gracious gift of tears.

It is a gift! Human beings are marked as different from the animals by comparatively few characteristics. And one of them is the power to know sorrow and sympathy. Let these be forgotten, or hardened by neglect, and the distance between the pressing jungle and civilization will be measurably shortened.

"Jesus wept." The tears which He shed in sympathy for His friends are forever an example and a challenge to His followers.

The second passage which records the tears of the Master occurs in St. Luke 19:41. The incident happened in Holy Week when the Cross stood immediately before Him. Jesus had spent the night following the triumphant entry into Jerusalem at the home of Martha and Mary. On Monday He returned to Jerusalem. On the way He stopped on the Mount of Olives from which height the entire city was spread out before Him. It was then that St. Luke says: "He beheld the city, and wept over it."

The city of Jerusalem was facing a desperate plight. The conquering Romans controlled every phase of her life, and exacted from her people huge taxes to support a vast kingdom. Such a fate for beloved Israel was a reason for grief by every Son of David. But the tears of Jesus were caused by something deeper than mere national loyalty. Something more important had happened to Jerusalem than an invasion by a foreign army. The people had forgotten their God! Jerusalem was supposed to be the most religious city in the world; her priests were numbered in the thousands. Two million pilgrims came within the Temple every year to observe the sumptuous rituals, and to pay the money which was needed to support the gaudy externals. But there was no righteousness among the people. The "pure and undefiled religion" of yesterday was something which belonged to a forgotten past.

Jesus had come with a message of hope and redemption. He had spoken words of eternal life which belonged both to individuals and to cities. His teachings promised salvation for the Holy City. But His words were scorned, His message was laughed at, and even then the authorities were plotting to take His life. It was at such a time that Jesus paused on the Mount of Olives to look across the Valley of Kidron to where the City of Jerusalem spread out in all its glory. No wonder He wept!

The city which brings tears to the eyes of the Master is not only Jerusalem of the First Century. It is any city in any generation which has forgotten the voice of the Prophets, and has spurned the challenge of the godly.

The French artist Paul Flandrin put on canvas the eternal message of the weeping Christ in his masterpiece, "Christ Mourning Over the City." Christ is pictured as weeping as He looks down on a metropolis; but it is a city far removed from the setting of ancient Jerusalem. Crowded tenements are in the foreground. A great unlighted cathedral looms in the background, unlighted as if to tell of the spiritual darkness which engulfs the city. All the ignorance, and doubt, and spiritual neglect of the teeming cities of the world have been portrayed on the canvas. And yet the challenge belongs especially to Western civilization. It is the so-called splendor of Western civilization which has produced the great centers of poverty, and degradation, and spiritual neglect.

The change from old Jerusalem, with its vital faith in Jehovah, to the Jerusalem of Jesus' day can be traced by the historian. The change from strength to weakness in the cities of the Western world is even more easily discerned and, because the world moves faster, the tragedy unfolds more quickly. The spirit of godly men who built a city with a dream in their heart, and faith in God as their guide, is easily replaced when a people grow careless of the eternal values and abiding truths. "Politicians of Western nations ought not to be eligible for election until they have travelled in the ancient world," wrote H. V. Morton in his "In the Steps of St. Paul." "They should be made to see how easy it is for the constant sea of savagery, which flows forever around the island of civilization, to break in and destroy. Asia Minor was once as highly organized as Europe and America today: a land of large cities whose libraries and public monuments were so splendid that when we retrieve fragments of this lost world, we think it worthwhile to build a museum to house them. Yet a few centuries of occupation by a static race have seen the highest pillars fall to earth, have witnessed the destruction of aqueducts that carried life-giving water from afar, and have seen the silting of harbors that once sheltered the proudest navies of the ancient world. I cannot understand how a traveller can stand unmoved at the graveside of the civilization from which our own world springs, or can see a Corinthian capital lying in the mud without feeling that such things hold a lesson and a warning, and perhaps, a prophecy."

Wherever the spirit of Jesus Christ grips the life of a country or a city, there progress has been made and the bells of human freedom have rung from a hundred towers. But where faith is neglected, and human values are scorned, and the test of material values becomes the final test of greatness — in that city there is laid the seed of destruction. In that hour the Master stands by as He did when hearts were young and faithful. But now the joy which comes from observing the lives of honorable men and godly homes has left His face. "He beheld the city, and wept over it."

III

The third mention of the tears of the Master occurs in a reference to His suffering and death. It is found in Hebrews 5:7: "When He had offered up prayers and supplications with strong crying and tears." The incident in the Garden of Gethsemane is described here by the author of the Book of Hebrews. Jesus had left the Upper Room and had gone into the Garden. There, with Judas even then leading the soldiers toward Him, He poured out His soul in heart-rending prayer. "He began," says St. Matthew, "to be grieved and bewildered." "He began," says St. Mark, "to be amazed and bewildered." Hebrews tells us that His prayer was "with strong crying and tears." Some interpreters of the Bible have insisted that this passage indicated a fear of death. But such an interpretation does not at all satisfy the facts of the case. The Gospel of St. John precedes these events with Jesus' great discourse in the fourteenth, fifteenth, and sixteenth chapters. They are not the words of a man who is afraid of death. They leave no room for a belief that physical suffering could turn Him into a man who trembled before the fact of death.

It was something deeper which inspired the prayer in the Garden of Gethsemane. A whole life work was at stake there. Jesus had walked among the common people with a message which transformed existence from a drab affair into a thing of glory. He had come with a promise that His followers would have life, and have it more abundantly. Those words had proved to be true when tested by men and women. Even on Palm Sunday the hope had flickered that what He had already done was enough to save men. And now the Cross loomed before Him. Is it strange that He should wonder whether His death could bring a miracle which His life and presence had failed to accomplish? Is it strange that He should question if His whole purpose was to be smashed on the rocks of priestly jealousy? A dream and a work of the years

[143]

stood in the balance. The best efforts of His glorious ministry seemed threatened with destruction. Who would not weep?

It is at this point that Jesus gives help to His followers who are caught in events which shatter their dreams, and lay in ruins the work of a lifetime. Many faithful and earnest Christians have wondered in hours of personal disaster or bereavement if some blind fate had not scorned the plan of the Creator. In such an hour it is easy, and human, to shed bitter tears.

But for Jesus there was a word which accompanied the tears. It was a pledge of confidence in His Father God: " Nevertheless, not my will, but thine be done." He was not spared the Cross, but His followers were to know the triumph of the Easter morn. The tears of despair gave way to the joyous laughter of victory.

That kind of victory has often been the experience of the faithful Christian. The late Charles Eliot, former president of Harvard University, was born with a birthmark which disfigured a large portion of his face. Few little ones have ever had a handicap which brought so many tears from a loving mother and father. Late in life he told of the day when he himself first became conscious of his handicap. He was then a small boy. He had gone out to play with some of the children of the neighborhood. Their cruel jeers sent him home to look into the mirror at his disfigured face. That day he knew the agony of human suffering. His tears were uncontrolled. The following morning his understanding mother led him apart. She took the hands of her son into hers, and spoke gently to him: "It is not possible for you to get rid of this handicap. We have consulted the world's best surgeons, and they say that nothing can be done. But it is possible for you, with God's help, to grow a soul so big that people will forget to look at your face. Do it, son. Begin today."

Charles Eliot followed his mother's injunction. He became honored and loved by men of learning in every part of the world. The tears of personal disaster were replaced by the joy of achievement.

Such a victory often occurs when human dreams crumble in the dust. I know a gallant lady who lay for years on a hospital bed. Her body, strapped to a hard, wooden frame, was seldom free from racking pain. She often wept the tears of suffering. Yet she lived with a constant assurance of God's love and care.

The words telling of the tears which the Master shed under the shadow of the Cross can be a source of encouragement to His followers in every generation. It is not weakness to weep. It is not strange for the child of God to shed tears when his best dreams and hopes have crumbled. But it is a glad privilege for every Christian to know the victory of God's purpose when the final reports have been gathered and filed.

Indeed, it is the wondrous experience of the follower of Christ to discover again and again that the occasion which inspired the tears became the doorway to a more abundant hope in the days as yet unborn.

> We look through gloom and storm-drift
>   Beyond the years:
> The soul would have no rainbow
>   Had the eyes no tears.

The tears of the Master become, then, a pledge that God Himself is not spared the hour of sorrow; but, even more, they are the assurance that tears are wiped away when the divine purpose has its full expression in the life of His followers.

IV

Tears! The Master of Men knew them. He, too, walked the way of sorrow which His followers have trod in every generation. His tears were shed in sympathy for the suffering of others; His tears were shed because of the godlessness of the world; His grief was seen in the hour of personal tragedy, but with a foretaste of triumph shining through the tear-dimmed eyes.

This is a generation which has known more weeping than any generation in the history of men. The homeless and destitute of the world are numbered in the millions. Death has become a daily experience in countries torn by war. The cries of men must not be empty, selfish screams of pain. Followers of Jesus Christ are privileged to know that an hour of tears is often a gateway to a new and abundant life.

CHAPTER XIII

The Body of the Master

Text: " This is my body." — *Matthew 26: 26*

"TAKE, eat; this is my body." What familiar words! They have been spoken in great cathedrals, and in tiny chapels. They have been spoken by ministers and by priests, by bishops and by popes. They have been spoken in hundreds of languages and dialects. "Take, eat; this is my body." Christians have only fragmentary information concerning the physical appearance of Jesus, but the idea of the body of the Master has meant something real to His followers in every generation.

Throughout the centuries of the Christian era the symbolism and faith of the church has emphasized the spiritual body of Jesus. Such an emphasis, important and practical as it is, should not obscure the facts about His physical body. It was that body which made a home for His glorious spirit. It was that body which was buffeted by the crowd in Jerusalem. They waited throughout the night for an opportunity to jeer and scorn Him. It was that body which bore the load of the Cross, and which was nailed cruelly to the symbol of degradation. It was that body which bore the pain and anguish of the terrible hours when earth's worst horror was heaped upon Him. It was that body which at last grew limp in the silence of death.

There is no evidence that the Disciples considered the body of Jesus to have special significance in the days when they walked the Galilean road with Him. They did not seek to protect Him from the pressing crowds which drained His strength. They seldom showed concern that He receive the proper food and rest. When Mary sought to give special honor to His body by the pouring of oil and ointment upon Him, they gave silent approval to the rebuke of Judas Iscariot.

It was only after the Crucifixion was over and done with that His followers showed a special interest and concern for His physical body. Each of the Gospels records the fact that Joseph of Arimathea secured His body from the Roman authorities. They are precise and definite in their description of the incident. St. Matthew and St. Luke both say that Joseph " went to Pilate, and begged the body of Jesus." St. Mark says he " craved the body of Jesus." St. John reports that Joseph " besought Pilate that he might take away the body of Jesus."

Each of the Gospels tells of the careful preparations which were made for His burial. St. John says that the myrrh and aloes which were used to treat His body were "about an hundred pound weight." The linen clothes and spices with which He was honored were worthy of a person of the highest position and influence. It is evident that, whatever the neglect during His lifetime, the physical body of Jesus came into its own after His death.

I

But the growing Christian Church has never felt entirely at ease when the theologians have attempted to perpetuate the physical body of the Master through the celebration of the Last Supper. Martin Luther was the father of Protestantism, but the larger portion of the Church accepted Zwingli's spiritual conception of the Sacrament in preference to that of Luther. The Doctrine of Transubstantiation has disturbed many Christians. We have turned away in revulsion from a belief which sought to make the followers of Jesus partakers in the eating of His actual physical body rather than sharers in the mighty spiritual experience born of Christian fellowship.

We Christians have been on firm ground when we have emphasized the habits and practises which help to keep us spiritually healthy. It is the idea of the supremacy of the soul, rather than the body, which is essential to a victorious Christian life. By such an emphasis we are walking in the path laid down by our Lord.

Early in the Gospel of St. John the writer reports an incident which reflects the attitude of Jesus toward the physical body. He had been speaking of His power to destroy the temple, and in three days to raise it again. It is then that the writer adds: "He spake of the temple of his body." For Jesus the human body was a temple, made sacred by the fact that it housed the soul of man. For its own sake the physical body had no significance. Its importance lay in the fact that God had made the body the means by which the spirit of man was given opportunity and place to grow. Frederick Lawrence Knowles reflected the Master's attitude toward the physical body in unforgettable words:

This body is my house — it is not I:
Here I sojourn till, in some far sky,
I lease a fairer dwelling, built to last
'Til all the carpentry of time is past.
When from my high place viewing this lone star,
What shall I care where these poor timbers are?

What though the crumbling walls turn dust and loam—
I shall have left them for a larger home!
What though the rafters break, the stanchions rot,
When earth hath dwindled to a glimmering spot!
When thou, clay cottage, fallest I'll immerse
My long cramped spirit in the universe.

[151]

What a change in the attitude of Christians toward death would occur if the conception of Jesus were to become the faith of His followers! What a change of attitude would be observed in many burial services. Death has stilled the physical body. And now what is left behind? Only a shell; a body empty of the only thing which gives it lasting significance.

The early Church quickly caught Jesus' understanding of the relationship between the physical body and the spirit. Much has been made of a few passages in Scripture which seem to indicate that the writers conceived of the Judgment Day as a day when the physical bodies of all faithful Christians of every age shall be restored to the form in which they last appeared at the time of death. Few more horrible thoughts have ever clamored for acceptance. By far the larger number of passages in the New Testament assert the unimportance of the physical body. Paul declared that "we are . . . willing rather to be absent from the body, and to be present with the Lord." Or again he asked: "Know ye not that your body is the temple of the Holy Spirit?" If, then, the spirit be gone home to God, of what use is the temple?

In many parts of America there are tiny country churches which are now closed and barricaded. Once they flourished, and were crowded with worshippers. But the population has changed. Now they are desolate and forlorn reminders of another day. There is but little spiritual inspiration in a reminder that these discarded buildings once were churches. A church is made significant by the presence of people who bow before its altar to worship. When the worshippers no longer find the presence of God in that spot, there is nothing to inspire the traveller who passes by. It is so with the temple of the spirit. The physical body is important and holy because it is the agency through which the power of God is given to men. Let the spirit leave the body, and the body has lost its true reason for being. Let it then be laid away in honored rest, or let it be unrecognizable as the Unknown Soldier in time of war — it matters not at all.

Jesus gave a further emphasis to that attitude when He said, " Be not afraid of them that kill the body, and after that they have no more that they can do." For Jesus the body had no significance in itself. Let the body be killed, and the only essential part of life still remained. It is the destiny of that essential part of life which must be of greatest concern to the followers of Christ.

II

This attitude of Jesus toward the physical body prevails not only in the hour of death. The recognition of the true significance of the spirit is triumphantly possible, and necessary, throughout life. His teachings concerning this important matter focus on two great facts.

1. Jesus tells His followers that they should "take no thought for their body." He was concerned lest men should give the whole of their time and interest to the pursuit after the things which could satisfy only the body. To give added emphasis to His argument He told the story of a man who had great possessions, but who was dissatisfied even with his abundant material fortune. He continued to seek after riches. When success crowned his efforts he had no room to store his wealth. "This will I do," he said; "I will pull down my barns and build greater." Then Jesus gave God's answer to the man: "Thou fool, this night thy soul shall be required of thee." Of what use then was the provision which had been made for his body?

Citizens of the Twentieth Century have struggled as have those of no other generation to secure bodily satisfaction. Professor P. A. Sorokin in his epic study "The Crisis of Our Age" marshals impressive facts to indicate that the struggle has ended in failure. He reminds us that "we turn into money and profit any value — quintuplets, scientific invention, religious revivals, novel crime, and what not. Successful money-makers compose our aristocracy." Yet the striving has been in vain, for, at the end of the wild era there was not a rainbow, but the worst war which ever took the united efforts and lives of mankind.

The late Dan Crawford, one of the greatest of Christian missionaries to Africa, reported that he

[154]

talked to an African chief concerning Christianity. He described the glories of civilization for him, with its mighty cities and scientific wonders. The old chieftain seemed strangely unimpressed. He listened calmly to the end, and then asked solemnly, "But are your people happy?" Dan Crawford declared that he gave a quick answer in the affirmative, but later he was not so sure. He wondered if the people in the western world were happier because of their bodily satisfactions.

It is a question which must always probe and disturb the faithful Christian. Jesus said, "Take no thought for your body." What then would He say to the people who have used their mightiest efforts for no other cause except to develop means by which the common man will be able to work less, eat more, and spend more time doing nothing? What would He say to a people who confess Him to be their Lord, but who spend more time watching the lurid picturization of moral filth on the screen than they do in worshipping in the House of God? What then would He say to a people who spend more time with how they look and what they wear than they do in making a soul of beauty? Would He not thunder out again to say, "Thou fool, this night thy Soul (not thy Body) shall be required of thee"?

To the men and women of this generation who are surrounded by the gadgets and appliances which contribute to make bodily satisfaction the word of Jesus is difficult to accept. Yet note this! It is His Word: "Take no thought for your body."

2. Jesus declared that what happened to the spirit was in large measure the determining factor as to what would happen to the body. In the Sermon on the Mount He said, "The light of the body is the eye: if therefore thine eye be single, thy whole body shall be full of light." Let the eye see life with a look of faith and power, and the body is filled with the fruits of faith and power. If the eye looks with fear and uncertainty upon the events of life, then the body is racked by uncertainty and fear.

A girl of nine was recently brought into a nearby Child Guidance Clinic. From her earliest childhood she had been unable to walk in a straight line. She would make a circle about six feet in diameter, always returning to the point from which she had started. As she grew older, and had more strength for walking, the problem became serious. The desperate parents took her to doctors and specialists. They took X-rays and made various laboratory tests. Their efforts were of no avail. They could find no physical weakness to explain the tragic pattern. Because the fact of human equilibrium rests on minute adjustments in the inner ear, the doctors were certain that some minor physical weakness had escaped them. The reason for the peculiar handicap, they felt, must be explained by some imperfection in the physical body. Then, more as a desire to help the child to make an adjustment to her environment than with any hope of assistance in the difficulty itself, the parents took the little girl to the Child Guidance Clinic.

After only a few visits to the clinic the reason for the difficulty was established. As a toddling baby a pattern of fear was set in the child's mind. The escape from the cause lay in a return to her mother's arms. The circle which she continually took when she tried to walk became the return to a place of refuge and security. When the mind had been cleared of the dark forebodings the body then reacted in a normal way.

The human mind is an intricate and mysterious organ. Its relation to the soul has never been clearly established. Many of the best known psychologists have asserted that the soul and mind are closely related, if not identical. Jesus of Nazareth was aware of the power of mind to influence and control the physical body. Over and over again He stressed the importance of keeping the mind clear to receive the message of God. He told His followers that it mattered not at all how strong the body was if the mind were so weak as to yield to evil.

Miss Grace Moore has rightly earned a place among the great sopranos of history. In her autobiography she tells of the first occasion when she tried to sing in Switzerland. The setting seemed perfect. The piano was well placed, and was played by a skilled artist. Her training and background gave every evidence that she could sing with power. She took her place by the piano, listened to the introduction, and then opened her mouth to sing. But no sound came! There was absolute silence. Panic-stricken, she turned to her hostess for an explanation. It was then she learned that the high altitude had affected her voice. The atmosphere did not yield itself to song.

Men are often equipped with strong and healthy bodies. Their environment seems to have provided all that is necessary for happiness. Yet they are unable to play their full part in life. They are tortured by fears and uncertainties. The atmosphere in which they live does not yield itself to great character.

The human body is fearfully and wonderfully made. It can and should be strong enough to meet the pressing demands of even the most taxing responsibilities. That men are dominated by fears and moral weaknesses is a certain sign that the mind has lost its contact with the Divine Source of power and guidance. Jesus was eager that His followers should live triumphantly. Such a triumphant life does not depend on the size or power of the physical body so much as it does upon the manner in which the mind links up the power of God with the needs of every day. Christ promised that when such a thing happened, " the whole body will be full of light."

III

Early in the history of the growing Church, the body of the Master came to have deep and abiding spiritual meaning for His followers. Such a truth came to its fullest expression in Paul's letter to the Church in Corinth when he said, "Now ye are the body of Christ." This passage is not the only such conception of the continuing body of Jesus. Paul was inspired with the idea. In Colossians he tells of "the afflictions of Christ in my flesh for His body's sake, which is the Church."

Such an attitude toward the body of the Master is in keeping with Jesus' teachings concerning the physical life of man. The body for Him was no more than the home of the soul, and the means by which the soul may develop the qualities which have eternal worth.

The Church then is Christ's continuing body. The voice of the Church is His voice; the hands of the Church which do His service of healing and ministering are His hands; the feet of the Church which carry the message of faith across the world are His feet; the eyes of the Church which search out the places of greatest need are His eyes.

Arise ye, then, O Christian! Yours is a mighty heritage, and a mightier responsibility. The Master awaits your Christlike deeds that He may come alive in this generation. The Church is the body of Christ.

Chapter XIV

The Mind of the Master

Text: "Let this mind be in you which was also in Christ Jesus."
— *Philippians 2: 5*

THE Apostle Paul expressed a breathtaking confidence in people who had caught the spirit of Christ. His words constantly throb with a mighty hope for men whose lives are consecrated to God. Nowhere in spiritual literature is man's triumphant destiny so clearly visioned as in the words with which he challenged the Philippian Christians: "Let this mind be in you which was also in Christ Jesus."

Paul's assumption that it is possible for the followers of Christ to have minds like the mind of the Master is an unparalleled tribute. It is easily conceivable that fellowship with the Master might be so intimate that the look of His eyes, or the sound of His voice could be seen in the lives of His followers. Men tend to imitate the walk, or voice, or smile of someone they greatly admire. But the mind of the Master is different! It stands in a place of supremacy above every other characteristic of His earthly life.

Paul fully appreciated the greatness of the mind

of Jesus. He never failed to pause in awed silence before the name of Christ. No man ever exalted Christ more highly! Yet he wrote to the Christians in Philippi: "Let this mind be in you which was also in Christ Jesus." We turn the pages of the Gospels with eagerness to understand what really was the nature of the mind of the Master.

Manifestly the Gospels contain no case history of Jesus' mental life. Students of religion have frequently speculated concerning what a few hours alone with Jesus might have revealed to a modern psychiatrist. A few have suggested that an examination of His mind would explode the idea of His Divine Sonship, and totally dissipate His significance for the human race. To the earnest student of the Gospels such a point of view is ridiculous. The mind of the Master is clearly revealed in the Scriptures. Questions concerning His physical appearance still remain unanswered, but the wonders of His mind are a vital part of the Christian heritage.

What then do we know about the " mind of Christ?"

I

First, the mind of the Master held His body under firm control. His body was to an amazing extent dominated by His mind. Jesus was able to endure great physical privations. That fact is made clear in the Gospels. He needed less rest than His Disciples.

He was still on His knees in prayer while they lay in an exhausted sleep. He was awake on the mountain in the early morning while they still remained on their couches. But the record also reveals that He died on the Cross long before the accustomed time for victims of crucifixion. Even Pilate wondered why He died so soon. The records indicate that His body, in life as in death, was the servant of His mind.

The fascination which the life of Jesus exerts over His followers is due to the welling forth of His wondrous and unique mind more than to any other single fact. The deeds of His hands, and the events with which He is associated, all have their place in the history of those days; but it is His mind which continually challenges His followers. No other life in history flowed so completely from an inner strength. As Friedrich Rittelmeyer so aptly said, "Nothing external left any mark on Him, but the whole external world has come to bear the imprint more and more of the quality of His inner life."

Prior to Holy Week Jesus had been following a daily program of teaching and healing which strained His energies to the breaking point. But the hardest days were still ahead! As if the threat of imminent death were not enough, He was faced with the unfaithfulness of His followers. Then came the crowning physical strain of slow death by the most tortuous method known to man. Through it all there was no flinching, or desire to escape. He kept to the end the calm and untroubled spirit which had indelibly impressed Pontius Pilate. His mind was triumphant over every physical trial.

This quality in the mind of the Master has often been found in His followers. The frailties of the body have frequently been mastered by the Christian mind. John Milton, writing at a time when blindness had seemed to write an end to a brilliant career, said:

> The mind is its own palace, and in itself
> Can make a heaven of hell, a hell of heaven.

It must have seemed like an invitation to the depths of despair when the darkness closed about Milton. He proved to the world that the mind is able to build a place of refuge in the vale of human tragedy.

John Wesley demonstrated during his lifetime that a mind fired by the Divine Presence is triumphant over every physical ailment. Alexander Knox wrote concerning Wesley's final weeks on earth as follows: "So fine an old man I never saw! The happiness of his MIND beamed forth in his countenance. Every look showed how fully he enjoyed the gay remembrance of a life well spent."

When Bishop Hannington was put to death in Africa on October 11, 1885, the cause of missions in that continent suffered the greatest loss since the passing of David Livingstone. The manner in which he

[163]

endured suffering, and faced loneliness, betrayal, and cruelty constitutes one of the most inspiring stories in Christian history. But his happiness in the midst of pain was an even more impressive fact than his courage. He marched to death singing " Safe in the Arms of Jesus." Bishop Tucker, his successor, said of him, " This remarkable man has been beaten, imprisoned, put in a chain gang, had his house burned down and his property destroyed; yet he has borne it all with a smile upon his face and a song upon his lips." Bishop Hannington gave to all Christians an example of the manner by which the mind may control the body.

The mind of the Master dominated His body. He never was a slave to the needs of the flesh. Suffering and disappointment left their marks upon His body, but His mind remained unscarred. The Apostle Paul recognized the fact that anxiety and fear were defeating many of the early Christians. He therefore challenged them to " let the mind be in you which was also in Christ Jesus."

II

In the second place, it is essential to know that the mind of the Master dwelled on facts of faith rather than argument. Whoever looks to the Gospels for an atmosphere of thinking totally detached from the world will be disappointed. Many of the theoretical

[164]

questions which confound the modern seeker after truth are ignored. There is no formal attempt to relate the doctrine of the love of God to the problem of evil in the world. Jesus does not argue the existence of God, nor does He try to relate the omnipotence of God to the idea of human freedom. There are none of the abstract reflections on human experience which characterize the teachings of Buddha, or Confucius. His mind lived in a world of faith rather than argument.

Compared with the entire breadth of human thought, Jesus' teachings are merely a small segment. But note this! He spoke with assurance and power concerning every essential factor in human experience.

The intellect has an important place in the religious life of man. The need to interpret Christian experience in the light of the newest scientific knowledge was never more necessary than in our generation. Jesus was impatient with a religion which depended on rites and ceremonies. His mind would revolt against intellectual sham in our day as violently as He reacted against the Pharisaic sham of His day. Yet He would be equally impatient with an attempt to make the intellect an end in itself. God can easily be lost in argument; the power of prayer can be dissipated in psychological analysis; the redeeming love of God can be retarded by too continuous a contemplation of the world's evil.

The mind of the Master did not escape the doubts which, across the centuries, puzzled men. In the Garden of Gethsemane and on the Cross He had moments of questioning. But these stand out by reason of their uniqueness. For the remainder of His glorious ministry, Jesus spoke words of positive assurance concerning His mission and the nature of His Heavenly Father.

Men today are not interested in exhibitions of mental gymnastics by earnest Christians. The expression of doubt concerning God and His relation to life no longer casts a spell over an audience. Bewildered searchers for truth now say, "Away with your doubts! Consider them in the silence of your own mind. Tell us what you believe! What do you know to be true?"

The mind of the Master was concerned with faith rather than with argument. Such a mind should be found in His followers.

III

The mind of the Master had an amazing grasp on what was real and essential in life. The writer of the Gospel says, "He knew what was in human nature. . . . He knew." Indeed He did! When Matthew was seated in the taxgatherer's booth there was nothing in his outward appearance which gave reason to expect he might respond to noble things. But the mind of Jesus recognized something more. The Scripture dismisses the matter with the statement that "He saw a man." Jesus' eyes looked on the man, but His mind saw the unexpressed longings within him. Matthew was forever different because the mind of Jesus understood the long-buried dissatisfaction with his life.

He did it on many occasions. In those who seemed most unworthy He recognized hidden qualities and undeveloped abilities. On the other hand, beneath the silken robes of the Pharisees, His mind uncovered the hidden sham and dishonesty.

His mind captured and held men. The Centurion came to Jesus and found nothing in His dress and environment to indicate that the Master was of peculiar power. What was it, then, which led him to adopt the manner of a servant before his ruler? It was the mind of Jesus which left the proud Roman with the indelible impression that he was in the presence of a person of peculiar power.

The hold of the mind of Jesus on the lives of men did not end with His earthly ministry. Beginning with Paul, the pages of Christian history glow with the accounts of men of great influence, as well as those of lowly estate, who have been held firm by the mind of Jesus.

Even men who doubted His divinity, and spoke disparagingly concerning His earthly life, have been unable to escape the enduring power of His mind.

"Don't worry, Katie," wrote D. H. Lawrence to the late Katherine Mansfield, "Jesus is a back number." But Lawrence was held by the power of Jesus down to the end of his life. He went back again and again in his letters and in his essays to discuss the Man of Nazareth. Usually he was slow to praise and quick to condemn. But the mind of Jesus held him with a grip of iron, and he could not escape.

Many of the people who stirred His greatest interest were dismissed by those about Him as of no importance. Macaulay wrote of Horace Walpole: "The conformation of his mind was such that whatever was little seemed to him great, and whatever was great seemed to him little." That kind of mind was worthy of the mind of the Master. Jesus was always more interested in what was within a man than in what appeared on the surface. He recognized that men could live in big houses, and still have a soul that floundered in the gutter. He knew that people could be dressed in silken garments, and still be clothed in the veil of sorrow. He knew that men could walk proudly along the road of respectability, and still grovel in the alleys of sin.

His mind was never shackled to events as they appeared about Him. He always looked ahead to the time when doubters would see the light, and when the Kingdom would have its deserved place in the life of men. It was that way with the Cross. If Calvary had been finished and done with at three o'clock on Good Friday, the life of the Master would probably have held little significance for men. It is not strange that the Disciples were willing that afternoon to mark off their experience with Jesus as a failure. Their despair is understandable. But the mind of the Master had peered beyond the Cross to the hope it held for the world. He knew that His hours of suffering would hold men from evil, and keep them firm in their struggle against the same forces which had brought Him to the Cross. The mind of Jesus was able to pierce the veil which hid the future and find there a reason for the struggle.

Such a mind must rule His followers in this generation. Gone are the days when men or nations can live a year at a time. God's world will be destroyed by hatred and fear if the mind of man is not adequate to plan for a century of peace and security.

There is hope here! If the hands of Christians are consecrated to the task of doing God's will; and the voices of Christians are ready to speak His message of assurance and hope; then the minds of Christians should be able to look into the future and build a world worthy of his dreams.

Alfred Lord Tennyson's mind penetrated the future in the spirit of the Master. His words in "Locksley Hall," written seventy-five years ago, are prophetic of the devastation wrought by the modern airplane. Even more remarkable is his dream of what may happen in coming generations. He wrote:

For I dipt into the future, far as human eye could see,
Saw the Vision of the world, and all the wonder that would
    be;
Saw the heavens fill with commerce, argosies of magic sails,
Pilots of the purple twilight, dropping down with costly bales;
Heard the heavens fill with shouting, and there rain'd a
    ghastly dew
From the nations' airy navies grappling in the central blue;
Far along the world-wide whisper of the south-wind rush-
    ing warm,
With the standards of the peoples plunging thro' the thunder-
    storm;
Till the war-drum throbb'd no longer, and the battle-flags
    were furl'd
In the Parliament of man, the Federation of the world.

The mind of the Master looked far into the future. He saw both the hopes and dangers which were to confront His followers. Such a long view of life is essential today. Paul lifted his voice in challenge to the early Christians. Hear him as he says to people in our day as well: "Let this mind be in you which was also in Christ Jesus."

IV

Finally, the mind of the Master was fed by eternal things. The hours He spent in prayer were as necessary to His ministry as was the more material food which Martha prepared for Him. Concealed from our view are the hours in His life when He retired to renew with fresh stores the original power He had received from God. We know that Jesus gave much time to God alone, however much time He was called upon to give to men. And there are suggestions in the Scriptures that those who loved Him were aware that He was in a state of mighty power when He came back from the hours on His knees. When He came down from the mountain, on one occasion, His Disciples broke out almost as with one voice with the request, "Master, teach us how to pray!" After the hours spent in prayer in Gethsemane, He went out to meet His enemies. It will be recalled that His presence reflected such power that they fell back at first as from a conqueror.

The mind of the Master was fed by eternal strength which came from hours spent in prayer. Such spiritual food is an even greater necessity for His followers who desire to live triumphantly in this generation.

The mind of the average Twentieth Century citizen has but slight acquaintance with the Presence of God. Men speak of the "crowd" mind, and we understand what that means; it is a mind motivated by the desire to do what the crowd does, and to gain the approval of those in the social whirl. Men speak of the "movie" mind, and we understand what that means;

it is a mind moulded by the ideas and standards of contemporary motion picture performances. But the "Godly" mind, or the "Eternal" mind is comparatively unknown. The undergirding of life and purpose by the power of God makes possible an inner triumph for all Christians who have such a mind.

On a blazing hot day in Jerusalem I saw a demonstration of how men can face disaster when their minds have been strengthened by eternal resources. It was a few hours after bloody riots had brought death to more than thirty people. A crowd had gathered about the hospital to wait for an announcement of the names of the victims. Anxious parents and wives hurried forward each time the door opened. After one such announcement a sorrowing procession moved slowly down the street. In the center of the group was a woman who had just been informed that her husband was one of those killed. She moaned and screamed so loudly she could be heard far away. In her grief she was supported by two aged men who walked, one on each side of her. Suddenly one of the men addressed her sharply in a foreign tongue. Immediately her weeping ceased. A friend standing nearby translated the words which brought the sudden change. "The old man said, 'Be not so weak! Do not forget that we still have God!'" A mind which had been steeped in the knowledge of God could face both disaster and death.

The mind of the Master was fed with eternal food. By the power of His God-filled mind He became "more than conqueror" over all that the world could do to Him. No one was ever more conscious of the mind of Jesus than was the Apostle Paul. He salutes all of us with words which are both a promise and a challenge: "Let this mind be in you that was also in Christ Jesus."

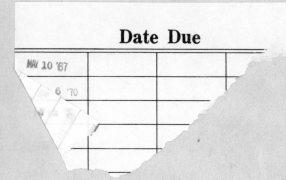